THE FAITH OF MEN

Books by the same author:

Atheism in Our Time
The Authentic Morality
The Ways of Friendship

THE FAITH OF MEN

Meditations Inspired by
Teilhard de Chardin

by Ignace Lepp

Translated by: Bernard Murchland

THE MACMILLAN COMPANY, NEW YORK

First published in France by
Editions Universitaires, Paris, under the title of
Teilhard et la foi des hommes.

Library of Congress Catalog Card Number: 67-24287

First Printing

The Macmillan Company, New York
Collier-Macmillan Canada Ltd., Toronto, Ontario

PRINTED IN THE UNITED STATES OF AMERICA

Contents

THE FAITH OF MEN

Introduction

The following essays are inspired by the works of Teilhard de Chardin. But I am not sure that he would see his influence in all of them. Nor do I doubt that "orthodox" Teilhardians, more concerned for the letter than the spirit of writing, will disagree with much of what I have to say. But isn't it characteristic of exceptional men like Teilhard de Chardin to offer something to those who seek truth who are very different from one another? For many years, I found my most substantial spiritual nourishment in his then almost "clandestine" writings. Such nourishment gradually became my own substance. And this is what I would like to share with my readers. They may not agree with all the points I set forth, but I hope that they will at least be encouraged to go directly to the master himself and find nourishment in his work.

My conversion to Catholicism, at the age of twenty-seven, had little to do with the doctrinal or intellectual content of Christianity. At a particularly critical period of my life, I was moved by the heroic generosity and the warm brotherhood of the early Christian communities as I knew them through translations of such historical novels as *Quo Vadis?* by Sienkiewicz, *Fabiola* by Cardinal Wiseman, and later on, by reading the original works themselves. I also read the Gospels, numerous books on the life of Christ (notably that of Ernest Renan), the *Fioretti* of Francis of Assisi, and biographies of the saints. In a word, Christianity first impressed me as an existential rather than a doctrinal reality.

Once a Christian, I needed to bring my faith into accord with my intellectual needs: *fides quaerens intellectum*. But I must admit that the study of scholastic theology, far from illuminating and consolidating my faith, only disturbed me. Its syllogistic reasoning, its constant and insistent reference to an outmoded cosmology, its vain disputations, if not quite on the sex of the angels, at least bore on the different kinds of grace and the like. I could not see how any of this had any relationship to the Christianity of the Gospels and the saints. And I certainly could not see how such a theology could promote the evangelization of the modern world, particularly that part of the intellectual world whose outlook I understood best.

Most of the theological works that were recommended to me during my early years in the Church were far inferior to the vision of the universe revealed by modern science. The geocentricism (and underlying anthropology) of these works immediately repelled me, while the syllogistic demonstration of scholasticism was unable to convince me of anything, or demonstrate a single truth. Moreover, a hymn that was popular at that time, "I Have But One Soul To Save," seemed to translate only too well the spirituality of the majority of Christians I knew. It seemed to attach too much importance to our small, individual selves. I was quite unmoved when I read Pascal's remark to the effect that Christ had shed such and such a drop of blood for me personally. To be sure, I had high regard for my own individuality and that of others. But as a young student in philosophy, I had found my intellectual joy in Plato. Later on, I adopted Hegel as a master, without renouncing the former, however, whom I still consider the greatest of all philosophers. In a word, as a result of the joint influence of Plato and Hegel, but probably also due to a deep personal intuition stimulated by my first questions about the world, mankind, and myself, I became deeply convinced of the primacy of the whole over the individual. I have and will never be able to consider humanity as a simple juxtaposition or as an aggregate of individuals bound together by a social contract. Quite the contrary, I have always seen humanity as the first reality; individuals, including myself, were only partial and contingent realizations of it. Christ, in my opinion, could only have shed His blood for all of humanity, and it is only because I belong to mankind that I, too, can hope for redemption.

I also read the writings of the Christian mystics: Thomas à Kempis, St. John of the Cross, Tauler, and many others. All seem to put too much stress on individual salvation, upon the relationship between God and the solitary soul. This kind of intimacy struck me as unnatural. The "palpitations of the heart" and "mystical marriages" related by some of the most venerated saints in the Church made me very uneasy. Of course, I knew they were symbols; but these kinds of symbols embarrassed me, and I knew they could only embarrass most of my contemporaries who had not been brought up in the Catholic seraglio. Father de Lubac initiated me to the thought of the Greek fathers—Gregory of Nyssa, Basil, Gregory of Nazarene, and the Alexandrians. Their outlook was infinitely more universal than Western writers. But the official masters of the Church ignored the oriental doctors, suspecting them of "Neo-Platonism" (which, in my opinion, was far more valuable than the poorly integrated Aristotelianism of the theology manuals).

At this critical moment in my Christian life, an old priest who taught theology in Lyons gave me a mimeographed copy of a book called *The Divine Milieu* by a Jesuit paleontologist, unknown to me, named Teilhard de Chardin. I have often reread and meditated upon that marvelous book; it presented exactly the kind of synthesis of Christian spirituality and modern needs that I myself more or less consciously needed. Little by little I came across other books by the same author: *The Personal Universe, How I Believe, The Mass of the World,* and several others. I can say without hesitation that they determined the course of my spiritual life. Because of Teilhard's works I was gradually able to realize, for better or worse, the indispensable synthesis between my Christian faith and my "natural" convictions and knowledge. That synthesis has never been broken or even seriously endangered by any of the crises I subsequently experienced. Much later, during his stay in France before he was "exiled" to America, I had the great privilege of knowing Father Teilhard de Chardin personally. My familiarity with his work, which is to say with the life of his powerful soul, was then such that we became fast friends.

It would be obviously pretentious to say that Teilhard offers the only way of salvation for Christians today. I know many fervent believers, including some who are highly educated, who find the traditional works of Christian spirituality quite adequate to their needs. Still others are seriously troubled by reading Teilhard. Nonetheless, it is my experience that a great many educated men and women today find insufficient spiritual nourishment in the past treasures of Christianity. To be sure, these treasures are in themselves inexhaustible and always contemporary. If they are unable to satisfy so many of our contemporaries, it is not because the latter are too intelligent or too superior to be content with the spiritual food of the past. We no longer bask happily in the complacent optimism of the nineteenth century when it was customary to refer contemptuously to the "darkness of the Middle Ages." In the past half-century, educated people have become, by the force of events, much more modest. I remember as a child hearing my grandfather, who was a fanatic freethinker, speak with undisguised indignation of the horrors of the Spanish Inquisition and the religious wars. In his opinion, those times had gone forever. The "darkness of the past" had given way to the "rational light" of the present. None of his grandchildren, however rationalistic they might be, would dare make such a statement.

Modern man, then, cannot claim any radical superiority over preceding generations. At the same time, it would be a serious error not to recognize the radical difference between mankind today and mankind of the past. I think one of the reasons why anguish and confusion are so pronounced today is because teachers and spiritual directors have not been cognizant enough of this difference. Let us recall St. Paul's admonition to provide food adapted to the age of the recipient. This is true for historical man as well as for individual man. An Eskimo does not require the same kind of food as an African; the intellectual must eat differently from the laborer. The same is true of the food for our souls and minds.

In the course of the past two centuries, man's situation in the world has been radically transformed. The man of the seventeenth and eighteenth century was probably psychologically closer to the man of Greek, Roman, Hebrew, and even Egyptian antiquity than to twentieth century man. For thousands of years, to take but one example, the world and the universe were taken to be practically synonymous. Even after Galileo and Christopher Columbus, most men continued to think, act, and react as though Aristotelian cosmology were the only conceivable one. Minor changes were admitted; but in the main, the educated man remained convinced that he enjoyed an absolutely unique place in the universe and that his privileges were not seriously threatened. The theologians disputed at length whether or not the Indians of North America were among the redeemed; they finally agreed upon the Asiatic origins of the American tribes and thus solved a problem that seemed in the beginning beset with insurmountable difficulties.

How different is modern man's image of the universe! Astrophysics and nuclear physics have completely changed our outlook. On the one hand, man is presently in possession of unprecedented power over the forces and resources of nature. At the same time, he feels infinitely small and impotent before the immensity of the universe. When he reflects upon his position in the cosmic scheme of things, it is difficult for him to avoid vertigo. It is impossible for him to feel secure. And from a psychological point of view, intellectual insecurity is as dangerous as material insecurity.

It was inevitable that the gigantic upheavals that changed man's situation in the world also would change our conception of God and the adoration due Him. Neither the national God of the Hebrews nor the anthropological God of the Middle Ages any longer corresponds to the spiritual demands and practical experience of our times. As late as World War I, most French, German, and other Christians found it normal when their priests identified the cause of God with the cause of their country. I don't know a single Christian today who would consider the war in Algeria, for example, a religious crusade for the cause of God. Some rightist circles still speak of the need for a crusade against "diabolical communism," which they identify with the antichrist mentioned in the Apocalpyse. But Pope John XXIII, in his different messages, has probably made this kind of exploitation of religion for political ends henceforth impossible. I know German Christians who were very sympathetic to Hitler's cause and even today believe that their former behavior was justified. Yet none of them would admit having prayed to God for the triumph of Naziism. Perhaps some of them did. But they now regret it, for history has made it abundantly clear that the God of the Gospel is neither German nor French, neither conservative nor liberal. He is simply the God of universal love.

Given these conditions, it is easier to understand why it is difficult for us to be satisfied with the spiritualities of past centuries. We still read Tauler and Suso, John of the Cross and Theresa of Avila, Fenelon and Margaret Mary Alacoque. We may even experience a certain esthetic-religious pleasure in reading them. But despite their great influence in the past, they are of little help to us in our effort to live and act as twentieth-century Christians. All of these eminent masters of the spiritual life emphasized the individual relationship of the soul with Christ and God. "Me and my God," was their general motto. Such individualistic mysticism no longer excites the man who thinks and reflects upon himself and the world. Individual man seems so small and insignificant in a cosmos that unveils its immensity before our astonished eyes. Only a truly cosmic mystic is capable of reaching the minds and hearts of educated men today. This, of course, in no way denies the individuality of each human being. But we are more and more inclined to consider the rights and duties of the latter in reference to a whole of which we are a part.

The mystics of the past spoke almost exclusively about the salvation of the soul. They attached little importance to the body. Today we are so convinced of the substantial unity of the human person that we would like the priest, at the moment of eucharistic communion, to say that the sacramental body of Christ is a pledge of eternal life for our whole person and not just our soul. Cardinal Saliège, who was an eminent theologian as well as a Christian leader, went so far as to speak of "holy matter" and called himself a "Christian materialist"—a conjunction of words which would have horrified Christians of the nineteenth century, to say nothing of those of the eighteenth century.

During the last two centuries, a veritable abyss has opened up in Christian spirituality between the terrestrial and the celestial, between the temporal and the eternal. The progress of the natural sciences has demonstrated the immensity of the terrestrial and temporal domain. Christians, at first unnerved by this revelation, could see no way of integrating the new universe with their traditional conception of the world. They thus abandoned the terrestrial and the temporal to the laws of mechanics and resigned themselves to a schizoid attitude according to which the good Christian should concern himself with what pertains to the eternal and heaven. Those who wished to explore the universe, to know it and glorify its beauty were soon forced to break with Christianity. The abyss that separated the "children of the earth" and the "children of heaven" continued to deepen, so much so that it seemed inconceivable that one day a bridge could be built from one to the other.

It took a long time for Christian thinkers and leaders to realize that their disinterested attitude toward the world had disastrous consequences for spreading the Gospel's message. They had become temporally inefficacious. Because of their absenteeism, the modern world evolved outside of the direct influence of Christianity, so much so that philosophers and sociologists have honestly been able to offer a definition and a description of the modern world without the least reference to Christianity. Yet isn't it obvious to all believers that Christ also redeemed this modern world? A religion that proclaims the Incarnation as its central dogma can tolerate such a division between the temporal and the eternal only at the risk of denying itself. Parallel to the new Christian awareness, many worshipers of this world and social progress came to realize that a too exclusive adoration of the temporal is in the long run very inadequate and unsatisfying.

It is symptomatic, especially for one accustomed to thinking dialectically, that the realization of the harmful effects of a too radical separation between the supernatural and the natural came about in a special way in France. For after Descartes, this separation was most pronounced in France, reaching at times Manichaean proportions. As of 1830, Lamennais and the small group of Christians involved in the journal *L'Avenir* recommended a reconciliation between the modern world and Christianity for the greater good of both. But the immense majority of their co-religionists were unable to understand their intentions and hastened to defend the old values, which they mistakenly took to be eternal. Nonetheless, the pioneers of *L'Avenir* had opened the way, and fifty years later Marc Sangnier and *Le Sillon* was much more sympathetically received by the Christians of France. Parallel to this effort on the political and social plane, other Christians began the work of building bridges between Christianity and the modern world at other levels. The naturalist Pierre Termier together with the poets Charles Péguy and Paul Claudel sang the beauties of creation and man's sublime mission to collaborate in the advent of a divine creation. Henri Bergson elaborated his celebrated doctrine of creative evolution and provided proof that the theological concept of creation and the scientific concept of evolution, far from contradicting one another were complementary. That Bergson's work was judged dangerous by the Church and placed on the Index is evidence of a time and a spirit that can only embarrass a Christian today. Large numbers of educated men owe the beginnings of their faith in Christ to Bergson.

These attempts to reconcile Christianity with the modern world failed in the final analysis. The two were still generally considered to be closed systems. Some form of compromise between them might be hoped for, but nothing more. A real and living synthesis could only come from a man who was both an authentic Christian mystic and deeply in love with the world. This historic mission fell to the Jesuit Pierre Teilhard de Chardin, a universally known paleontologist who played an important part in the discovery of the Peking man and the African origins of the human race. Scientific academies throughout the world were honored to count him among their members. Interestingly enough, this man who rendered such distinguished service to modern Christianity, and undoubtedly to the Christianity of tomorrow, continues to be suspected, calumniated, and opposed by the spokesman of his own Church. Yet the honorary committee presiding over the posthumous edition of his books included distinguished scholars from all countries, many of whom are far removed from the Christian faith. Teilhard's influence can only increase and shine more brilliantly as a result of this irony.

Is it because both came from Auvergne that one is automatically inclined to compare Teilhard de Chardin and Blaise Pascal? Their common origin in a province whose inhabitants have an almost legendary reputation for being down-to-earth pragmatists perhaps partially explains the fact that the two greatest modern French mystics were both scientists. The apology for Christianity that each elaborated was solidly based on positive scientific research. Before beginning his masterpiece, the fragments of which form the immortal Pensées, Pascal had gained fame for his treatise on conic sections, his writings on atmospheric pressure, the vacuum, the equilibrium of fluids, as well as for his discoveries of a calculating machine, the barometer, and other contributions that have long formed part of the common culture of mankind.

Most of the enthusiastic admirers as well as the fanatic adversaries of Teilhard de Chardin see him primarily, if not uniquely, as the mystic and theologian of modern times. His *The Divine Milieu* was circulated privately for over a quarter of a century. This volume and some others are what the enemies of the great thinker oppose, calumniate, and denounce. It is possible that *The Divine Milieu* will become as famous as Pascal's *Pensées*; both are likely to provide spiritual nourishment for many centuries to come. But we should not forget that Teilhard, like Pascal, first gained world fame through his scholarly works. For more than a half-century, he explored the prehistory of the earth, observing the evidence of primitive humanity in China and Ethiopia, in South Africa and Oceania, in America and in India. True sons of Auvergne, which has given France so many grocers and hotel keepers, Pascal and Teilhard de Chardin realized in their work and life an admirable synthesis between the highest mysticism and the most rigorous scientific spirit, between the terrestrial and the celestial. As we have indicated, there was an urgent necessity for such a synthesis in the modern world.

As a psychologist, I cannot but notice certain important differences between the two scholars and mystics from Auvergne. Pascal was an invalid, with a strong disposition to neurosis. His vision of human nature, no doubt at least partially due to this condition, was pessimistic; his sympathies were naturally with a rigid Jansenism. In the last years of his life, he had nothing but contempt for his own scientific achievements. His faith was uneasy and anguished; his celebrated "wager" betrayed an astonishingly superficial conception of religion, all the more surprising in that we know his love for God was deep and authentic. Pascal did not believe it was possible to love both God and His creation with a same love. He felt constrained to choose between them. He died at thirty-nine before completing his masterpiece.

How different was Teilhard de Chardin! He enjoyed truly extraordinary psychic health. He was nearly seventy years old when I came to know him personally, but he was still a magnificent figure of a man! His optimism and enthusiasm were contagious. His height, his fine aristocratic features, and ironic but never cruel smile commanded admiration. In his spiritual writings, there is not the slightest trace of intolerance, no opposition between God and creation, between heaven and earth. He takes it for granted that the love of God postulates love of the world and that, conversely, the love of the world should lead to love of God. Few Christians are so liberated from Manichaean dualism. As he himself admitted, he believed in God because he believed in the world. If for whatever reason, he said, he could no longer believe in the world, his faith in God would be proportionately affected. He experienced no sentiment of fear before God; only love. His trust in God's goodness was so strong that his adversaries accuse him, apparently with some reason, of making no place for hell and eternal damnation in his Christian synthesis. In fact, Teilhard's Catholic faith was always perfectly orthodox. He denied none of the Church's dogmas, especially the articles of the Creed. But it has always been the case that one or another aspect of the total faith is emphasized in individual Christian lives. From the point of view of practical spirituality, Teilhard never considered God as a judge. He contemplated the end of life not from the point of view of the last judgment, but in the perspective of the completion and perfection of God's work, a perspective not unlike that of St. John's Apocalypse (cf. Chapter 22 in particular).

Teilhard de Chardin's religious optimism was obviously rooted in his own psychic makeup. But it also owes must to his scientific conviction of the grandeur and the finality of creation. When *Humani Generis* was published in 1950, I spoke to him about my discouragement. He answered with his usual quiet irony: "How young you still are! Think rather of what will be said about this encyclical in 50,000 years. It is a mere drop of water in the ocean of history. Only the Church historians will remember it. Never forget that we are still 'primitive Christians,' for 2000 years is such a short time in the history of the cosmos. We are only at the beginning of the evolution of the spirit." He judged everything from this point of view. He saw all of reality in the vertiginous perspective of universal evolution, which is to say, in the final analysis, *sub specie aeternitatis*. None of the many difficulties he encountered in life, neither the bad faith and calumny of many of his co-religionists, nor the lack of understanding on the part of his superiors, really bothered him. But he was not indifferent and certainly not cynical. He was very much part of his times, sympathizing with the sufferings and miseries of mankind, sharing the most generous, indeed the most utopian of man's hopes. To the end he was animated by an infinite trust in God and in the world. The last words he wrote were: "I go towards Him who comes."

At the beginning of the twentieth century, when Teilhard de Chardin was a young man, Catholic apologetics made much of Pasteur and a few other scientists who still called themselves Christian. A high wall had risen between religious belief and scientific knowledge. The theologians themselves tried to elaborate a "scientific apologetics" that had no reference to revelation. Their intention was instead to prove the truth of Christianity by means of historical and scientific arguments. It was customary to say: "At the moment I am speaking as a scientist (or a historian); later, I will round out my thinking with insights from Revelation." Teilhard had always considered such dualism intolerable. When he was still a novice with the Jesuits, he wanted with one inseparable desire to be a servant of God and an explorer of nature. He had decided to tolerate no wall of separation between his priesthood and his love of the universe. He wanted to be a scientific Christian and a Christian scientist. He was faithful to this ideal of his youth until the end. His need for the Absolute was no less than that of his compatriot Pascal. But he adored this Absolute everywhere and in all the forms he believed it to have in the empirical universe. "The world," he wrote, "is in the process of spontaneous conversion to a kind of natural religion of the universe which turns it unduly away from the God of the Gospel. This is its 'unbelief.' Let us convert this conversion itself by showing through the example of our lives that only Christ, *in quo omnia constant*—in whom all things are contained—can animate and direct the newly undertaken march of the universe. Out of today's unbelief will perhaps come tomorrow's belief."

Teilhard never wavered in his belief that the elite of today could never understand or admit a supernatural unless they saw it, not as the negation, but as the fulfillment of the natural order. The Christian who would bear witness to his faith must become a man in the fullest sense of that word. This conception clearly contradicted the current prejudices of the nineteenth century; nonetheless, it is in accord with the most traditional Christian teaching. Thomas Aquinas himself taught that there could be no supernature without nature.

Most scholars take little interest in daily life and are particularly indifferent to, if not indeed contemptuous of, political life. But Teilhard de Chardin followed the events of the political world with passionate interest. Political life, particularly in the years immediately before and following the Second World War, struck him as highly important for the advent of the noosphere, for the evolution of the Spirit. Always observing such events with scientific objectivity, he was nonetheless personally concerned by them; they engaged all of his rich emotional life. As a paleontologist, he was accustomed to viewing history not only in its immediacy but in the light of centuries as well. Communism, nationalism, socialism, fascism, liberalism, and other ideologies of his age seemed to him to be more or less important elements in the general cosmic evolution. This perspective more than anything else enabled him to remain an optimist despite the apparent triumph of the forces of darkness. Indeed, some of the events and ideologies that most of his contemporaries considered absolutely new and "modern" were from his prophetic point of view already outdated and for that reason no longer effective. He knew quite well that mankind was preparing for the worst butchery in history during the years 1930–1940; but this did not prevent him from holding out the ancient hope of a truly universal human community. He was a great paleontologist; but humanity's past was far from being a mere object of scientific curiosity to him. Knowledge was also a means of working toward a better future for mankind. By discovering the ways in which the present emerged from the past, he believed he could predict the laws and rules governing the emergence of the future. His chief ambition in life, which he articulated in the last period, was to gather together the world's most eminent scientists and thinkers in order to save the future of mankind from a threatening anarchy and promote it in function of a clear vision of finality. Like Einstein, Oppenheimer, and so many other eminent scientists of our time, Teilhard de Chardin was tortured by this question: Will men be able to dominate and direct the gigantic forces and new energies that science has put at their disposal? He was an optimist, but no utopian. He knew that modern science could accelerate the spiritual future of mankind. But he was also aware of the mortal danger implied in the abuse of these same discoveries. He was too well acquainted with the political circles of different countries not to realize that an effort would be required to avoid disaster. He thought that only the professional servants of the spirit, the scientists and thinkers, were capable of controlling the energies that they themselves had discovered. Teilhard thus addresses himself to economists, naturalists, and philosophers. It made no difference to him whether they were Catholics or Protestants, believers or unbelievers. His long experience with teamwork taught him that many so-called atheists are more devoted to the service of the spirit than the most fervent Christians. He was much more at home with men like Lord

Russell, Jean Rostand, Arnold Toynbee, and Julian Huxley than with narrow-minded and emotionally stunted Catholics. Could this international society of thinkers have become a reality had Teilhard not died? We will never know the answer to that question.

It goes without saying that a man whose passion for unity was as intense as Teilhard de Chardin's could admit no artificial separation between intellectual reflection and the spiritual life. His whole work and life proves that he was at once an eminent scientist, a profound Christian thinker, and a genuine mystic. Few men were as qualified to make theirs the words of the psalmist: "Heaven and earth proclaim thy marvels." God must be known and loved through His creation. In Teilhard de Chardin's mind love of the world is simultaneously and inseparably love of creation and the Creator. His life's work was an effort to liberate Christian mysticism and spirituality from the influence of Manichaeism, from the ancient dualism between the human and the divine, the world and heaven. He always categorically refused to admit that one had to renounce becoming a man in the fullest sense of the word in order to be a true Christian.

The controversy over Teilhard de Chardin's person and work that has taken place within Catholicism seems to me due to a serious misunderstanding. Nor do I hesitate to say that there was a good deal of bad faith on the part of his adversaries. Most theologians were formed in the tradition of systematic Scholasticism. Christian revelation was presented to them as a whole that was forever closed and fixed and capable of furnishing an indisputable answer to any possible question. It was the professor of theology's role to tell his students what the Church taught as truth; in no case could he seek new ways that might permit a better understanding of Revelation. But the protagonists of this method are quite wrong to consider it traditional. Neither Origen, nor Basil, nor Augustine, nor Thomas Aquinas feared to open new avenues to an understanding of eternal truth. The reason why Christian theology became a static system is to be sought in the decadent scholasticism of the late Middle Ages. Teilhard de Chardin merely broke with this false tradition. The Church and Christians owe him a great debt of gratitude.

Teilhard de Chardin did not declare war on this psuedo-tradition merely to give vent to his aggressive spirit. In plain fact, it was impossible for him to act otherwise. Any man with a modicum of scientific education today instinctively rejects ready-made systems, for he knows by experience how unlimited and infinite the truth is, that there is always something new and deeper to be discovered. No scientist would dare pretend that he knows everything, or attempt to elaborate a *"summa"* of all knowledge, even within his own speciality. The modern scientist is more aware of his limitations than his predecessors.

Teilhard de Chardin was an authentic scientist. He never pretended that he could provide a definitively satisfactory answer to all the questions that confront Christians. In his writings, he speaks only of the questions with which he was existentially confronted. He believed that he was capable of giving an answer that could satisfy the intellectual demands of the contemporary, educated man. Thus, although it is true that he speaks little about hell and original sin, his enemies are wrong to conclude that he denied these dogmas of the Catholic faith. His quasi-silence simply means that these were not problems for him personally, or that he did not think he could shed any light on them.

Well aware of the spiritual thirst of men who were outstanding by reason of their knowledge and generosity, Teilhard de Chardin worked all of his life to project a new Christian apologetics capable of attracting such men to Christian revelation. Unfortunately, ecclesiastical authorities proved themselves incapable of understanding or approving this project and consequently Catholicism still lacks a format for presenting its doctrine in a way that can satisfy men of a scientific mentality. Happily, the writings of Teilhard de Chardin and his disciples are there to at least partially fill this need. But it is clear that they do not have the approval of ecclesiastical spokesmen; quite the contrary, the Administrative Church is highly suspicious of them.

The disciples of Teilhard de Chardin do not consider all of his hypotheses or intuitions definitely established truths. To do so would be to lose the right to call oneself a disciple of Teilhard, for all dogmatism was foreign and even antipathetic to him. What we can and should admire in this thinker is his love of truth, his perseverance in research and, above all, his unswerving fidelity to Christ. Neither misunderstandings nor persecutions on the part of his co-religionists and superiors could shake his faith.

Probably nothing bothered Teilhard de Chardin more than to

observe frequently that many Christians were humanly inferior to many unbelievers. To pretend to be an authentic Christian without striving first of all to be a real man struck him as an absurdity. "Why is it so difficult for Catholicism to cease being a sect?" he wrote. "How is it possible for nine Christians out of ten to be skeptics as men? This is a great scandal to the Gentiles." Despite this, he remained firmly convinced that only Christianity, on the condition that it was properly understood, is capable of stirring the spiritual energy of the universe. One is not a Christian for his individual salvation, but because he holds the Church to be "phyletically" indispensable for the fulfillment of mankind in the Cosmos. Teilhard would have rejoiced in the ecumenical style of John XXIII. This pope's trust in Christian truth's power of attraction—so great that he wanted to put an end to traditional doctrinal condemnations and extend his hand to all men of good will—is the very essence of Teilhard's vision.

In my first enthusiasm for Teilhard de Chardin's works, I prophesied that he would surely be declared a doctor of the Church by the year 2000. I still believe that the influence of his work on the scientific age is comparable to the influence of St. Augustine on antiquity and St. Thomas on the Middle Ages. I know only too well from personal experience how differently men today think than in previous generations. After geocentrism was renounced, the anthropology based on it also had to be renounced. We may well admire the systems elaborated by the early doctors of the Church, but it is psychologically impossible for modern man, and for much greater reason men of the future, to find in them the kind of spiritual food he craves. Yet we are convinced that the message of Christ is addressed to the men of today and tomorrow as well as to those of the past. Even non-Christian thinkers now recognize that the modern world has found no substitute for Christian mysticism even though all civilizations require some such universalist spirituality. Some, like André Malraux, have given up all hope and resigned themselves to a world without a soul. Such resignation is unacceptable to Christians. We believe that only the externals of Christianity have become outmoded, but that the essentials are always and eternally young. I personally think that the modern world, so immense by comparison with the little "worlds" of the past, is in urgent need of Christ's message of love.

Many think Pierre Teilhard de Chardin has best understood the spiritual needs of modern man. He also discovered the path that must henceforth be taken by the apostles and apologists of Christianity who hope to be truly efficacious.

Although I still retain my initial enthusiasm, I no longer believe that Teilhard de Chardin has much chance of being proclaimed a doctor of the Universal Church. Not merely because he was misunderstood by ecclesiastical authority; that was also the case with Augustine and Aquinas. The principal obstacle is in Teilhard de Chardin's work itself. It is not concerned with all that has been traditionally expected of a doctor of the Church. Neither Basil nor Ambrose nor Augustine were conformists. Thomas Aquinas had his difficulties with the Index, and the mystical doctor of the Church, John of the Cross, was sent to prison by the "holy" Inquisition. Nonetheless, they were all less radical innovators than Teilhard de Chardin. This is aggravated by the fact that "traditions" have become more and more rigid since the Counter Reformation, and this puts Teilhard in the light of overthrowing them completely. It seems to me that of all Teilhard de Chardin's predecessors he best compares with Origen. Origen is not a doctor of the Church either, although the Church probably owes more to him than to many official doctors.

The spiritual similarity between the Alexandrian of the third century and the French Jesuit of the twentieth-century is unquestionably a close one. Origen was the first to attempt a Christian synthesis. Until that time, Christian books were addressed to simple men with little education. Origen saw the urgency of Christianizing the intellectual elite of the Greco-Roman world as well. Since he had no predecessor to guide him, he did not always clearly express his religious experience and intuition. The narrow-minded and suspicious thus had little difficulty in detecting "heresies" in his writings. For a long time, a violent controversy raged over the issue of "Origenism." Since the high Middle Ages, Origen has been considered the master of errors, and the faithful have been prohibited from reading him. Only in recent times have French and German theologians undertaken a serious study of his writings and discovered with joy that the first Christian theologian was truly a genial thinker, that the "Origenism" so long denounced by the theology manuals had little in common with the teaching of Origen himself.

Teilhard de Chardin knew little about Origen. Nevertheless, the similarity between them exists. Teilhard saw the present scientific age as the beginning of a new era in the spiritual evolution of the universe—to such an extent that, in his eyes, this age is so markedly different from preceding eras that its truths can only be incomprehensible to men of today and tomorrow. Thus, any reference to medieval theology can only harm Christian revelation. Origen was obliged to expound a Christian vision of the universe within a world that drew its intellectual inspiration from Neo-Platonism. Teilhard de Chardin set himself an analogous task within a rationalistic world that draws its intellectual inspiration from the natural sciences. Thus, it is easy to understand why he encountered bitter opposition. He had, for example, to create a new terminology that is frequently difficult to understand and can lend itself to embarrassing misunderstandings. Yet it remains true that this terminology may be more comprehensible for Christians of the year 2000 than the concepts that are presently employed in catechisms and theology manuals.

Both Teilhard de Chardin and Origen are noted for their imperturbable optimism. Both are accused of not taking a human nature wounded by original sin sufficiently into account. As a matter of fact, Origen was hard pressed to make a place for the eternity of hell in his Christian vision. Since God is incontestably love, he dared believe that at the end of time Christ would offer all of saved creation in homage to His Father, including Lucifer, the fallen angel. Teilhard didn't go that far, for he was aware that the Church had defined the dogma of hell's eternity precisely to counter Origen's optimism. Nevertheless, the idea of hell is quite foreign to his conception of God and creation. He was undoubtedly aware of this and that is perhaps why he avoided comment on these subjects. I think I am right in formulating his thought in these words: "Since the Church, in which I believe, teaches the existence of hell, it must exist. But I may hope that there is no one in it, otherwise the Redemption would not have been entirely successful."

The quarrel that presently divides the enthusiastic followers and the fanatic enemies of Teilhard de Chardin is as intense as the controversy that formerly divided those who were for and against Origen. We may hope, however, that Teilhard will receive justice sooner than did Origen. Teilhard de Chardin will go down in the history of the Church more as a prophet than a doctor. It is even very probable that his writings, which we admire so much, will not be the cornerstone of the theology of the future. Even his most admiring disciples are willing to admit that he was not qualified to assume this role. For example, he was much more familiar with modern sciences of nature and man than with Holy Scripture or the works of the Church Fathers. Yet knowledge of these is indispensable to anyone who aspires to renew theology. The new should not abolish the old; it should perfect it. But this much seems certain: Teilhard de Chardin has opened the only possible avenue to theological reflection in our new age. He will not likely be the Thomas Aquinas of our times—rather, its Descartes. Any Christian thinker who hopes to be understood and accepted by the modern world ought to know the path Teilhard indicated, even if he is not in agreement with his theories and hypotheses.

It is too early to attempt an assessment of Teilhard's influence on modern Catholicism. Until recently, his influence was felt chiefly in France. During the last period of his life, he often spoke with enthusiasm of the extraordinary renewal of French Catholicism. He seemed not to be aware that it was due in an appreciable measure to his own work. Not all Catholic leaders in France have read him by any means. But they are familiar with his name and some of the principal ideas expressed in his work. Scarcely thirty years ago, it was common to hear professors and other apostles of "reason" fulminate against the "shadows of religion." It was taken for granted that Catholicism was the sworn enemy of progress and science, the ally of reactionary and conservative forces. That kind of counterapologetics is rare today. And again substantial credit must be given to the influence of Teilhard de Chardin.

There is another sense in which Teilhard may be considered a prophet. As we have already said, he was principally interested in the past history of mankind because knowledge of the past enabled one, in part at least, to predict the future. He did not consider the future as static, as something already given, which we merely have to discover. Nor did he claim any special "revelation" about the future. As co-creators with God, men should create their own future. But by virtue of his knowledge of the course already traced by mankind, the "scientific prophet" was in a position to divine the direction and the meaning of the evolutionary movement. For this reason, he could say many illuminating things about humanity's future direction. Because science has discovered the laws of general determinism, humanity today enjoys much greater freedom than in past ages. In spite of numerous reasons for discouragement, the optimistic Christian, Teilhard de Chardin, hoped that men, by reason of their growth, liberty, and power, would avoid setting off some fatal catastrophe and instead create something truly great and beautiful. "Life is before us," Teilhard de Chardin exclaimed prophetically.

This introduction should make the spirit of these meditations clear. This is not a work of exegesis or commentary; nor do we intend to touch on all the themes of Teilhard's work. Our ambition is a modest one: to permit those who are suffocating in the spiritual poverty and aridity of the age to taste the waters of a spring that is capable of satisfying their thirst.

1

Belief in God and the World

In one of his most beautiful books, *How I Believe,* Teilhard de Chardin wrote: "The originality of my faith has its source in two domains that are usually considered antagonistic. By education and intellectual formation I belong to the 'children of heaven.' But by temperament and professional training I am a 'child of the earth.' A natural synthesis developed between these two influences."

For one who adopts Teilhard's perspective, it is obviously scandalous that there are still Christians today who have no real love for the world. By force of circumstance they benefit from its riches and beauty, but they generally do so with a bad conscience. Love of the world is most often viewed by them as a kind of profanation of existence. They think that faith in God obliges them to center their life on something "higher" than the world. To love the world would mean in their opinion abandoning all aspiration to an authentically spiritual life and renouncing the "higher" in favor of the "lower." When they recall that the world is also the work of God, their faith is threatened by doubts and difficulties. They basically think that the world is neither beautiful enough nor perfect enough to be the creation of God. Without admitting it, such Christians fall squarely into Manichean dualism and attribute the creation of the world to some evil principle. In their intellectual and spiritual myopia they see nothing but ruin and failure in the world. They believe in God not because of the world but in some sense despite it. One of my patients in psychotherapy is an educated woman and a fervent Christian. The world seems to her so ugly and evil that she is victimized by an agonizing spiritual crisis. She forces herself to make an act of simple faith as a means of protecting her trust in a good and loving God. Nor are neurotics the only victims of such difficulties.

Some men, on the other hand, are passionate lovers of the world. They consider the construction of the world and its transformation in terms of mankind's ideal possibilities the highest mission of their life. To discover the secrets of the world and admire its beauty is a noble enterprise. Life in the world seems to them so beautiful and so self-sufficient that they see no philosophical or psychological necessity to postulate the existence of another life, of any kind of "heaven." We must admit that great numbers of today's elite belong to this category. Some of them rejoice in the discovery and liberation, the mastery and exploitation of nature's resources. It is an exhilarating experience to split the atom, to learn the nature of the distant moon and stars, to explore virgin forests and desert, to scale the heights of the Himalayas. Others experience a similar joy in tracking down the vestiges of man's early life on earth. Teilhard de Chardin reported with almost mystic elation the discovery of the Peking man and, later, the evidence for the African origin of man. A third category of the "children of the earth" dedicate themselves to the sociological transformation of the world and men. The Russian writer Ilya Ehrenburg wrote proudly: "Once there was a desert in central Asia; now gardens have taken the place of the desert. But we will do far more than this. We will transform men to such an extent that they will not recognize themselves." There is a good deal of poetic braggadocio in these words, all the more ironic in that the comrades of Ehrenburg's party have not yet succeeded in creating a new world that is better than previous worlds, or a new breed of superior men. But it is understandable that such Promethean pretension can give a meaning to the life of some of this century's finest men.

In any event, this much is clear: Whatever the form of modern man's love of the earth, there is no place in it for heaven or the supernatural. Those few who, out of fidelity to their family or schooling, still believe in the dogmas of religion generally divide their lives into two radically independent domains. Their "real" life consists of a passion for the things of this world; their faith is a Sunday decoration. Nor does the supernatural appear as a useless luxury only to the educated. Many ordinary men and women— workers, farmers, teachers, doctors, etc.—are in exactly the same situation. They are not considered atheists or agnostics; many are practicing Christians. After my conversion to the Christian faith, when I got to know what is called the "Christian world" a little better, I was both surprised and disappointed to learn how small a place religion occupies in the daily life of most Christians. Later, I was to learn that most converts had a similar experience. Some of them gave in to the temptation to follow the example of "cradle Christians" and relegate religion to a mere social function. Others fled the world to adore God behind the walls of a monastery or convent without having a real vocation in this life. Still others fell away from the religion that could not give them a renewed and deeper conviction of life in the world.

I could never tolerate this kind of separation between my faith and my love of the world. Doesn't man tend instinctively toward unity, both interior and exterior? Inner conflict, which is considered the result of original sin or some psychic malady, is as painful and contrary to our real nature as conflict with others. Reestablishing the unity broken by sin or neurosis is in my opinion a necessary condition for all who would aspire to an authentic life.

Complete exclusion of the supernatural from life and exclusive devotion to the world is one of the practical solutions to inner duality. Many men deliberately choose this way. However, it is my experience that the elimination of one of the constitutive elements of authentic existence is a false solution to the problem. Life is a dialectic; and dialectic negation does not lead to suppression, but to transcendence, to the reconciliation of opposites. What is so unfortunate is that most men do not act as they do, which is to say antidialectically, out of laziness or because they are afraid of making the effort to achieve a superior quality of life, but more simply because such a synthesis seems impossible to them. They declare themselves satisfied with what they hold firmly in their hands: the beautiful world. Unfortunately, this radical immanence is infallibly condemned to be imperfect and cannot satisfy a demanding heart or mind. The evolution of the world and human creativity are surely marvelous things. But they cannot be truly sublime unless they can be exempted in some way from the fragility and unreality that characterizes everything that is temporal. Only a faith that teaches that time is the workshop of eternity can effect the realization of a true and positive unity in life.

The Christian, who is obliged by reason of his vocation as an intelligent collaborator with God to tend toward a much greater unity than others, must courageously engage in the discovery of the eternal in the very heart of the temporal. He must not be troubled or held back by superficial contradictions. There can be no doubt for the Christian that God is the sole creator of heaven and earth. Because of this unshakable conviction we should be capable of seeking and discerning God's hand in all things. With many Christians, faith in God precedes and is the basis of their faith in the world. There is nothing abnormal in this. "Heaven and earth speak of God's wondrous works." But only for those who have already recognized God and adhere to Him. For these the world is so marvelously beautiful precisely because it is the work of God. How often have I heard them say: "If I were not firmly convinced that the world is the work of God, far from finding it admirable, I would consider it monstrously ugly because of its many contradictions."

The case is quite different for the real "children of the earth." With them, too, all new belief proceeds from a faith that they already possessed. In all normally developed persons there is a "basic belief," a kind of initial intuition, that forms the basis of all later convictions. In order to verify the authenticity of any of my present beliefs, I should be able to establish the legitimacy of my psychological evolution beginning with this basic belief or intuition. Only a radical scientism of the kind practiced in the nineteenth century could hold that all of man's convictions and certitudes are absolutely rational.

Long before I read Teilhard de Chardin, my basic belief was not in God, but in the world. In my youth, as a result of reading Kant and other idealists, I doubted the reality of the external world for a period of time, asking myself whether it could be distinguished from the incoherent images of my dreams. But this was a brief crisis that I quickly overcame. Since that time, the solid reality of the world has never been a problem for me. Great was my surprise after my conversion to Christianity to learn that many Christians considered the world to be a deceiving mirage that they treated with contempt. Believing that this was a real requirement of the Christian faith, I made a temporary effort not to believe in the specific reality of the world and not to love it for itself. My efforts proved useless, and I began to wonder whether I had any right to call myself a Christian. The reader can, consequently, understand my great joy when I read these lines in *How I Believe:* "If it should come about that I lost my faith in Christ, in a personal God and in the Spirit, I would continue invincibly to believe in the world . . . I live by this faith. And I feel beyond all doubt that when the hour of death strikes I will abandon myself to this faith." No doubt was any longer possible. The instinctive aversion I felt for all philosophies and spiritualities that doubted or denied the solid reality of the world was now fully justified. The world, the universe, was an absolute certitude for me. It was the Whole of which all individual beings were parts. I am well aware of our precarious and ephemeral existence in this world; but no doubt can taint my faith in the world taken as a whole. And, as Teilhard de Chardin so magnificently demonstrated in the remaining chapters of his book, this unshakable faith in the world, far from diminishing faith in God, constituted the best and most efficacious apologetics in favor of such a faith.

Belief in the world is, therefore, my *basic intuition,* one of those first principles that, according to the old realistic philosophy, needs no external proof. I need no proof to believe in the reality of the world, of creation, for I feel myself to be one of the component parts of it, one of the elements of the Whole. It is possible that my ability to grasp the immediate reality of the universe is more developed than in most men. Nonetheless, I have observed that only in extreme cases of neurosis is the capacity to react to the temporal and spatial synthetically, that is to say in such a way that the whole is grasped through and in the multiple, totally lacking.

I understand the universe as a whole to be a dynamic and evolutionary reality; all of its elements are in constant movement toward a given end. Philosophers and theologians may well dispute the matter. Pessimists will deny all real evolution, and optimists will exalt its grandeur. But for the man who has any ability at all to think scientifically, there can be no doubt: The universe does not cater to our individual happiness, but develops according to the laws of finality. If we observe the already long past of the world, it is clear that its evolution is no arbitrary matter. It tends toward an increasingly perfect spiritualization. When we exclude, for reasons of philosophical prejudice, the evolutionary character of the universe, then everything immediately becomes incomprehensible. The materialistic illusion proves to be existentially very dangerous, for it inevitably leads to the negation of a basic faith in the reality of the world. Creation and evolution must be conceived as a spiritual event. When God created the material world, He did not abandon it to its immanent "mechanical" laws until such time as it pleased Him to create man with a spiritual and immortal soul. This would mean that God, the eternal Spirit, would not have participated in the history of the world for millions of years. In a Christian perspective, such a hypothesis is unthinkable. On the other hand, modern scientists know the singular and marvelous manner in which the evolution of the universe took place, from the most informed matter to the highest and most complex forms of psychic and social life. This grandiose epic would be absurd and incomprehensible if we were to suppose that it was accomplished without any participation of the Spirit.

Thus, I see the evolution of the universe as primordially the growth and development of the Spirit, a Spirit that is at once immanent in and transcendent to the world. The various mutations and developments that have marked the history of the world can only be the work of the Spirit. But it cannot be maintained that the Spirit is the product of matter; only the contrary process can account for the the evolution of both matter and spirit. The world as a whole takes on intelligible form only if it is considered as the work of the transcendent Spirit.

Since I cannot possibly doubt the presence of the Spirit in the past and present of a world in the making, I cannot doubt its presence in future developments, that is to say the immortality of the spirit. Of course, I am speaking of a cosmic Spirit here. Later we shall see that a similar immortality must be predicated of the individual spirit. In any case, the immense evolutionary development of the universe is proof that evolution carries the spirit toward increasingly greater freedom and self-consciousness. I am not, to be sure, denying those facts, states, and events that Bergson designated as "relapses of the *élan vital*." Our generation, which has seen the cruelty of Stalin, the death camps of Hitler, and the atomic bombing of Hiroshima and Nagasaki, cannot share the naïve optimism of the scientists and philosophers of the nineteenth century. We cannot even hope that the foreseeable future will be exempt from similar relapses. Present efforts to conquer outer space fill us with pride in our condition as men, in the power of the human spirit; but it also makes us tremble with apprehension and fear, for we cannot ignore the possible uses that men will make of this extraordinary increase of their power. Nonetheless, however important and redoubtable the "relapses of the *élan vital*," they cannot conceal the general direction of evolution. Nothing authorizes us to set any limits to knowledge and love. It is not, therefore, conceivable that the spirit will one day die.

Knowledge and love of the universe does not furnish us with scientific proof that man is called to union with a personal God for all eternity. This is a certitude of faith, not of science. Yet it is in perfect conformity with my basic faith in the world. If I were to lose my faith in this personal eternity, my primary certitude of the reality of the universe would be seriously affected. It would be an affront to our intelligence to admit that the evolution of the universe has tended for so many millions of years toward the emergence of the spiritual life and self-consciousness only to relapse into nothingness. My whole being protests against a hypothesis that can only abase and humiliate reality and diminish its intelligibility in which I believe so firmly. Long before I became a Christian, I believed in the world. But I was also vaguely aware that there was something deficient in a world of constant becoming. For a long time, I believed that evolution reached its omega in social revolution; gradually, I came to see that revolution could not justify the marvelous evolution and ever-increasing spiritualization of the universe. Only after I understood the Christian message did everything become clear. Although it was not always easy to adapt to the Christian world and submit to the Church's discipline, I have never wavered in my Christian faith these past twenty-five years. It seems that somewhere in my unconscious lurked an unshakable conviction that if I renounced my faith in God, my faith in the world would collapse. And since I conceived of myself as an integral element of the universe, how could I still believe in myself if I no longer believed in the world?

As a depth psychologist, I have had frequent occasion to note that faith in God, faith in the world, and faith in oneself are intimately bound up. Because the neurotic is not sure of himself, that is to say he has no faith in himself, he cannot have an authentic relationship to the world nor real trust in God. If we succeed through therapy in normalizing the patient's relation to the world, there is as a result always an increase in self-confidence, and for Christians, God ceases to be a frightening tyrant. He becomes a loving father. But the cure can also begin with a rebirth of self-confidence, or even with the emergence of a more authentic faith in God. The other two "faiths" follow from this.

2

Evolutionary Creation

"We still find here and there in the world people whose minds are suspicious and sceptical as regards evolution," Teilhard de Chardin wrote in *The Phenomenon of Man*. "Having only a book knowledge of nature and naturalists these people imagine that the transformist battle is still carried on as in the days of Darwin. And because biologists continue to discuss the mechanisms by which species could have been formed, they imagine that biologists hesitate (or that they could hesitate without suicide) about the fact and reality of such a development."

When I was a boy, there was a good deal of talk about the monkey man was supposed to be descended from. My grandfather, was a fanatic rationalist, was fond of going to the cafés and boasting that he was a direct descendant of the orangutan. This scandalized most of his audience because they still believed the biblical teaching that each man was created by God himself.

Until I was 27, I frequented circles in which a belief in evolution and man's continuity with the animal species was taken for granted. I knew from my reading that the evolution-creation controversy was very much alive in the nineteenth century. But from my point of view, the creation hypothesis was as outdated as the belief that the earth was flat. Moreover, I supposed that in our "scientific age" even the deists themselves no longer contested the evident fact of evolution and the transformation of species. I was surprised to learn, after my conversion, that most Catholics did not accept evolution as a scientific fact.

I personally do not understand why or how the fact of having descended from a monkey or any other animal could in any way diminish the dignity of man. In the first place, I have always liked animals and experienced no emotional problem in professing a biological and spiritual relationship between them and myself. Nor do I see any good reason why this relationship could not be extended to plants and minerals. When I first read St. Francis' *Fioretti* it was obvious to me that when he called the wolf his brother and the spring his sister he was not speaking merely metaphorically or poetically. Moreover, I have never felt embarrassed by the possibility of having descended from a monkey. By the same token, I have never considered the offspring of aristocrats or the wealthy more worthy of admiration than the sons of peasants and workers. Heredity has little to do with human quality. Quite the contrary, I have always had great admiration for the self-made man, for men who succeed by virtue of their talents and efforts. Should I learn that I were a son of Jupiter I would be very embarrassed, because I could never be a god but only a man, and a very average one at that. But since I am firmly convinced that mankind had very humble origins, I can only rejoice and be proud of its extraordinary development. When I compare educated men of today with some animal or with such primitives as the Cro-Magnon and Neanderthal man or even with certain twentieth-century primitives in New Guinea and Central Africa, I can only form a very high estimate of man's potential. That god bestowed such possibilities upon His creatures seems to me infinitely more wondrous than if he had created man in the beginning with the genius of an Einstein or a Teilhard de Chardin. That most men are not spiritually mature doesn't discourage me in the slightest. We have not yet reached a maximal point of development. When I reflect upon my psychic, moral, and spiritual imperfections, I believe I am correct in considering them "relapses" of spiritual evolution in the strict Bergsonian sense of the term. But such deficiencies in no way authorize me to cease my efforts to become more perfect or forget the finality of a development that tends toward an ever-greater spirituality, liberty, and self-consciousness.

Who would deny that the "era of the spirit," which Teilhard de Chardin called the noosphere, signifies an entirely new stage in the history of the universe? Teilhard was of the opinion, however, that the passage from the hylosphere to the biosphere, from inert matter of life, was even more marvelous than the passage from the biosphere to the noosphere, from animal life to the life of the spirit.

We have every right to question the *how* of these various revolutions that have marked the past development of the cosmos and will no doubt characterize future development as well. The materialist tries to explain everything by the "mechanical laws" immanent to eternal matter. I find this explanation very unsatisfactory. Whence come these laws if there is no legislator? Can the marvels we witness in nature be attributed to chance? Even if the eternity of matter were an established scientific fact (which it is not), I think creative activity would still be necessary, otherwise we would have to give up once and for all the effort to find intelligibility in the universe and its development. The passage from the hylosphere to the biosphere and from the biosphere to the noosphere are at least as "miraculous" as the origin of primordial matter. Neither the one nor the other makes any sense unless we suppose, at least hypothetically, the intervention of someone we conventionally call "God."

But there is a further problem: In what fashion are we to conceive of God's intervention in the history of the universe? Genesis gives a marvelous account of the creation of the world. I realize it is cast in a poetic form. However, not one word contradicts the most certain of modern scientific truths. In the beginning God created heaven and earth; He then gave birth to the hylosphere, next to the biosphere, and finally, to the noosphere with the creation of Adam and Eve. Man's ontological kinship with nature is explicitly affirmed. Both man and the different species of animals were created out of the same earth. But the "breath" of the Spirit makes man into the image of God, an entirely new kind of creature.

It would be false to discredit the Biblical narrative on the pretext that it is an anthropomorphic account of cosmic history. Neither the Jews nor the first Christians were under any illusion about this. Only children and uncultivated people think that the Bible must be accepted literally or rejected out of hand. It would also be false to see in the Bible only fables, even though the sacred authors frequently used an imaginative mold to express their thoughts. In reality, the Bible presents truth in a symbolic form. And the truth of a symbol is as great as the truth of the exact sciences. The truth of the Bible's account of creation is primarily the continuity of the diverse spheres of reality. The simplest and most primitive prepare the way for more developed, more complicated, and more structured forms. There is no contradiction between my Christian faith and Teilhard's hypothesis according to which God created man, not from formless matter, but from matter that was already living and organized. Indeed, this hypothesis responds much better to my own spiritual needs. Genesis and modern science agree that creation—or evolution—advances gradually, by steps: hylosphere, biosphere, psychosphere, noosphere. What purpose would be served by the long and laborious passage to the biosphere if the psychosphere had sprung directly from the hylosphere? It seems certain, therefore, that the biological being of man was formed within the animal kingdom.

In fact the evolution-creation controversy should be situated at another level. Even the most traditional theology admits that the essential difference between man and the animals is not to be found at the biological level, but on the psychological level. Anthropologists have been unable to establish a precise physical borderline between the superior anthropoids and the primitive human races. Zoology cannot determine for certain if a given skeleton discovered in a prehistoric cave belongs to man or to the animal kingdom. Conclusive evidence can be provided only by the traces of the Spirit's activity. Artifacts, tombs, the most elementary signs of culture, constitute irrefutable proof of man's presence. Nor need there be any misunderstanding about what is denoted by the term "Spirit." Even in its most elementary forms, the noosphere represents a radical novelty in natural history.

Traditional Christian theology affirms that God created the human soul directly, and from this point of view we cannot speak of a "natural" preparation. But such eminent Christian thinkers as Blondel and Teilhard de Chardin were of the opinion that the soul also pre-existed germinally in the inferior forms of the biosphere. However, this seems to me to be a purely theoretical matter that concerns neither science nor faith. As a Christian believer, I see the hand of God in the spirit as in everything that exists, however He may have created it. Man is made in the image of God because he participates in the Spirit of God. But since all creatures owe their existence to God, they also in some sense reflect the image of God.

Today, we have some difficulty understanding why the "evolutionists" in the age of Lamarck, Darwin, and Marx considered the biological, and even psychological, kinship between man and the animals as an argument against the Christian conception of man as Spirit and the image of God. Still more paradoxical is that Christians let themselves be so influenced by the prejudices of the era that they felt obliged, because of this misunderstanding, to reject evolution altogether. My relationships with nature are necessarily modified by my belief that I belong to the noosphere; and therefore, I, too, am a partial reflection of the image of God. I have always felt at home with nature. As a Christian, my relationship with nature is much more intimate because it is founded on a deep love. I know now that it is the work of God, and I have learned to see in it the narrator of divine wonders. I am more convinced than ever that there is no rupture in the continuity between man and nature.

Although Christians and materialists agree in the observation of, and to a large degree the interpretation of the facts, their notions of universal evolution are widely divergent. This does not mean that the Christian is less an evolutionist than the materialist; the very opposite is often the case.

As a Marxist, I naturally believed in evolution. But I always had difficuty within that mechanistic perspective explaining the marvelous evolution of the universe. Many Marxist thinkers tried to explain it "dialectically"—thus hoping to avoid the difficulties raised by a purely mechanistic conception of evolution. I also professed the "faith in dialectic," for even then I held the dialectic to be a law of reason. I still think it quite capable of directing the sociological and psychological evolution of mankind. But it seems to me contradictory to speak of an "immanent dialectic" in matter, thus making it responsible for the evolution of the whole universe. In my opinion, those who hold this view have abandoned the domain of scientific evidence and created a new religion in which dialectic plays the role of God. Even as an atheist I had to cling to some God, even if it were called "dialectic."

In the course of my philosophical studies, I read Bergson's *Creative Evolution*. It came as a veritable revelation. I suddenly understood that universal evolution was not at all the mechanical development of something already given, but that something new is created at every stage. This marked the end of that paralyzing determinism that I learned from my teachers and found so unsatisfactory. In my books and articles, I tried to convince the Marxists that we should consider Bergson among the most progressive philosophers, and that his thought was a necessary complement to Marxist doctrine. But to no avail. Bergson was reputed to have spiritual inclinations; indeed, he was suspected of an idealism that was strenuously rejected by the disciples of Marx. The latter were aware of the inadequacies of the mechanistic explanation; but they realized that it was less dangerous for Marxist dogmatism than the open and dynamic dialectic of Bergson's spirituality.

I have remained an admirer of Bergson, and I will always be grateful to him for having liberated me from the narrow and suffocating bonds of materialism. Without him I would probably never have made my way to the Christian faith. He made me aware of the spiritual dimension of my life. Today, however, I prefer to speak of "Evolutionary creation" rather than "creative evolution." The evolution of the universe, as scientists understand it, is unquestionably creative; but it does not create in the proper sense of the term. Bergson deliberately spoke in a purely phenomenological fashion, and the first Christian thinkers to become his disciples—including Teilhard de Chardin—were quite right to interpret creative evolution as the scientific expression for God's creative activity. The non-Christian followers of Bergson, on the other hand, were also right in seeing creative evolution as a purely immanent process. When Bergson wrote *Creative Evolution,* he probably hadn't worked out all of his ideas concerning the nature of that energy whose creative activity he discerned at work in the universe. Twenty-five years later, when he wrote *The Two Sources of Religion and Morality,* he recognized God the creator at the heart of creative evolution. Thus, we are not faithful to Bergson in using the more precise expression "evolutionary creation."

Teilhard de Chardin's celebrated great uncle, Voltaire, thought religion was a good thing for the masses. He compared God to a clever clockmaker. Since clocks exist, the clockmaker must also exist. Since the world exists, someone must have created it, and this creator we call God. It is incredible how many catechisms still use this image as a demonstration of God's existence. All they really demonstrate is their own ignorance. When a clock has been made, it no longer needs the clockmaker. But is this the case with the world? Should we take Genesis literally and believe that God rested on the sixth day and abandoned the world to its proper laws, laws that He has established, but which are entirely immanent to the evolution of the world? Such a static conception of God's creative activity is much more akin to materialistic mechanism than to the God of Christian revelation.

In fact, God will continue his creative activity in the world until the end of time. "Did God first create the egg or the chicken?" was a question that many serious theologians of decadent scholasticism posed. It is not an entirely meaningless question. Certainly God is not the immanent energy of the universe, as some concluded on the basis of Bergson's philosophy. On the other hand, the world is not merely an emanation from God as the Gnostics believe. God's absolute transcendence over the whole cosmos cannot be questioned. Otherwise He would not be God. At least theoretically, nothing is lacking to His perfection. This would be true even if He hadn't created the world. As traditional theology holds: No necessity or inherent constraint obliged God to create the world. But given the creative act, it seems to us "logical" and "natural" when we recall the teaching of Revelation that God is love.

Thus the creative act of God is a continuing one. The Creator cannot be compared to a watchmaker. He is not separated from His work; He never abandons it to its own laws. It is important to banish all anthropomorphism from the concept of Creator. In this we are again following traditional theology. According to Thomas Aquinas, divine Providence is nothing other than the temporal continuation of God's creative activity. In any event, there is neither contradiction nor opposition between God's creative act and the immanent laws of the universe. It is precisely because God acts creatively within cosmic evolution that the latter is capable of creating something truly new and unforeseeable. We must not be deceived by surface appearances. Of course, scientists can discover and formulate causal "laws" to explain a given step of evolution. But these laws, it must not be forgotten, are formulated only *a posteriori*. Let us recall Bergson's theory of causality. It is only from an *a posteriori* point of view that we can consider one thing as the effect of another and suppose with some degree of certainty that the same "cause" will always produce the same "effect" under similar circumstances. Thus, in this perspective, it seems perfectly normal that the bisophere emerged from the hylosphere, and that the noosphere will be the crowning point of evolution. Let us imagine, however, that due to some miracle we were able to observe closely the hylosphere independently of its evolution into the biosphere. We might have studied all the laws of the hylosphere in depth, and yet not be able to predict the emergence of the biosphere with any degree of certainty and still less describe its nature. The same could be said of the biosphere studied independently of the noosphere. In both cases, we are confronted with a veritable act of creation.

Let us insist once again upon an obvious fact: To speak of evolutionary creation in no way diminishes either the creative activity of God or evolution. Quite the contrary. Humanly speaking, the creation of a static and definitively constituted universe would seem far less exciting than the creation of a universe that renews and transforms itself constantly, one that is capable of developing from the lowest rung of the hylosphere to the highest spiritual summits of the noosphere. Moreover, even if such an achievement were attributed to determinism and its mechanical laws, such laws seem more intelligent and powerful than the customary images of God as a watchmaker. In truth, the God who creates according to the laws of evolution is worthy of our highest esteem and admiration.

We have no plausible reason to suppose that God has terminated His creative activity, or that He no longer intends to create nothing great. It took the hylosphere and biosphere millions of years to develop. By comparison the noosphere, which has emerged recently, is so young that we can scarcely think that is has realized the creative potential intended for it by God. We think with Teilhard de Chardin that mankind has a long history before it. To be sure, we are in no position to divine the future achievements of evolutionary creation. But we can dimly perceive the "direction of history," that is to say the path that evolution will take as it tends towards its fulfillment.

3

Man and God as Co-Creators

"In my activity," Teilhard wrote in his masterpiece *The Divine Milieu,* "I adhere to the creative power of God; I coincide with it; I become its instrument as well as its living extension. The desire to succeed, a certain passionate joy in the work to be brought forth are an integral part of our fidelity as creatures." For all psychically normal men, these words ought to be self-evident; but they evoke much contempt and hostility in the Christian world.

I am still indebted to Bergson for my understanding of human activity. Later, Teilhard would confirm and deepen it. Shortly after my conversion to Christianity, I read the following in *The Two Sources of Morality and Religion:* "Creation appears as God's enterprise to create creatures, to enlist the cooperation of beings worthy of His love." According to philosophy, what is most noble in God's creative act, an act that is freely inspired by the substantial love Who is God, is precisely to have conferred on man the power of loving and to have thus made him His co-creator. His detailed study of Christian mystics led Bergson to conclude that the great love that animated them all was in no way passive, but tended by virtue of the very power it received from God toward action, toward creative activity. "Mystic love tends, with the help of God, towards the completion of creation," he wrote.

Before reading *The Two Sources of Morality and Religion,* I had already read many Christian works that spoke of the dignity of man. Several times I asked myself the question: "In what exactly does this dignity consist?" I have always been an evolutionist. In the fundamental truths of Christian revelation that I was just then getting to know, I saw absolutely nothing that contradicted the continuity between the animal species and man. I could not, nor did I desire to question man's superiority over the animals, even the most highly evolved. Yet I did not see very clearly just what this superiority was. Formerly, I had thought it was a quantitative difference, and that was easy enough to understand. But I knew that Christians considered man's superiority over other creatures to be of the qualitative order, and I had difficulty understanding that. To be sure, Christians spoke of the immortal soul with which man alone was endowed. But I was accustomed to thinking empirically and phenomenologically; if this soul was to mean anything to me, I would have to see its practical consequences.

Bergson gave me the explanation I was looking for. Man is qualitatively superior to all other creatures because he is God's co-creator. Later, I was to learn from Teilhard de Chardin that it is by means of this creative activity that the spiritualization and sanctification of our lives is effected. There is no opposition between the life of prayer and the life of work; our work itself should be a prayer. At the same time, I understood the difference between believers and unbelievers. It is not that the former live for heaven and the latter for this world. The Christian also lives for the world; but he knows that this world will find its final fulfillment only in heaven. He thus takes the same route as his unbelieving brother. Nothing human separates them. But where the unbeliever thinks he has come to the end of the road, the Christian continues to push onward. The accusation that we are disloyal brothers, that we are not sincerely engaged in the construction of the earthly city, is a false one. We are wholeheartedly in favor of the sociological transformation of the world, as well as the scientific exploration and investigation of the past, present, and future. We are as interested in all of this as our unbelieving brothers. The more, the extra that we hope for, in no way excludes the less, but integrates it. Transcendence is not the denial of immanence, but its fulfillment.

Does Teilhard de Chardin exaggerate when he writes that nine-tenths of practicing Christians today still consider human work a "spiritual burden"? "Despite the practice of right intention and offering each day to God, "He says in *The Divine Milieu*," the generality of the faithful obscurely think that time spent in the office, the studio or the factory is something that distracts them from worship." Perhaps Teilhard's percentage is a little high; but far too many Christians still consider work profane, as having nothing to do with their faith in the Trinity, the Incarnation, and the Real Presence. Pious souls see in work a distraction form "the one thing necessary," or like many monks, they look upon it as a means of penance and ascesis. The Catholic martyrology mentions many canonized laymen and sermons readily stress their exemplary value for those "Who live in the world." But when we examine this matter more closely, we notice that all these mothers, kings, workers, teachers, and doctors were honored because their lives conformed to a monastic pattern of spirituality and not because they entered intimately into the joys and activities of daily life. I recall reading the life of Blessed Anna-Maria Taigi (1769-1837) shortly after I entered the Church. She was a simple Italian woman, married to a brutish and drunken man and the mother of eight children. The hagiographer made much of her many visions and ecstasies and her great gifts of clairvoyance. But he was especially concerned to laud her for not taking sensual pleasure in her husband's arms, for yielding to him only because he demanded it and for the purpose of having children, that is to say for giving immortal souls to the Church. As I remember it, the author established a direct connection between Anna-Maria Taigi's sanctity and her renunciation of all terrestrial joys and pleasures. I also remember asking: Would it have been possible for her to have become a saint if she had had a sensitive and loving husband who initiated her to the profound joys of love?

The scandal of the priest-worker movement to the Christian world can be explained in similar terms. Their effort to realize the priestly vocation in and by manual labor ran directly counter to the deeply embedded prejudices of most Catholics. On the other hand, nothing is more normal and logical than Teilhard de Chardin's warm enthusiasm for the priest-workers; more or less consciously, he recognized in them his own conception of the priesthood. The same spirit can be seen in the important Christian Family Movement in which couples strive, often heroically, to realize their Christian vocation in terms of their conjugal vocation.

A Catholic writer I once knew often said: "Before God it makes no difference whether you dig potatoes or build cathedrals. Neither potatoes nor cathedrals will enter the kingdom of God; you will be judged uniquely according to your *good intentions*." Many Christians shared this view. This is probably one of the reasons why temporal progress has for centuries been in the hands of nonbelievers who share the widespread opinion that Christians are the enemies of social, scientific, and psychological progress. Yet for many centuries, Christians thought differently. Indeed, they were the heralds of human progress at all levels. As is well known, it was generally believed in the tenth century that the world would end in the year 1000. But the Christians of that time did not act like latter-day prophets of doom who abandon all constructive activity and await the return of the Lord in prayer. On the contrary, the Christians of the tenth century wanted to make the earth as beautiful as possible for the Lord's coming. They built many beautiful churches, and the great Roman religious art was elaborated principally during that time. What impresses me is that these churches were no mere temporary structures, but have survived the centuries. This is exactly how I conceive of the authentic Christian attitude toward the world and history.

The Christian should respect every form of work and honor the humblest worker. All who work are in their way doing something holy and agreeable to God. As Teilhard de Chardin has written in *The Divine Milieu:* "From the hands that knead the bread to those which consecrate it, the great universal Host should be prepared and offered with *adoration.*" He spoke of the "mass of the world" in which all the efforts of all men would contribute to the consecration of matter, spiritualizing it and in some sense divinizing it. The final result is no more the work of the priest who pronounces the words of consecration than it is of the peasant who sows the wheat. The man of a single talent can fulfill the will of God by exercizing it. In this sense the aforementioned writer is undoubtedly right. But a man of great gifts who squanders them would scarely be worthy of our admiration. It is after all better to build cathedrals than to dig potatoes. There is an objective hierarchy of human activities, the highest obviously being those that are most immediately in the service of the end. The Peking man would not have been discovered without the arduous labor of those Chinese workers who moved tons of earth. Yet we rightly attribute the discovery to Teilhard de Chardin and other scientists who directed the excavation and interpreted its results. Let us recall the evangelical parable in which Christ severely reprimanded the servant who buried the talent that had been confided to him instead of multiplying it. We may suppose that the Master would have been much more severe with the servant who had been given five talents if he too had buried them.

About fifty years ago, during the so-called "modernist crisis," many men of good will who were seeking the truth encountered serious theological and historical difficulties with Christian doctrine. Were the Gospels really written by the Apostles? Did Christ really live in Palestine during the Roman occupation, or was He merely a mythical figure? Was Christianity as we know it today founded by Christ and His apostles, or was it invented by some such prestigious and enlightened preacher as Paul of Tarsus? There questions passionately interested our fathers, but are of little concern to educated men today. A half-century ago men like Loisy, Renan, Harnack, and others were regarded as prophets of a new era. But no one reads them today, and the young scarcely know their names. I once recommended their books, recently so well-known, to students who were interested in the problem of religion. They found them insufferably dull and unquestionably out of date. Modern man is, in fact, much less optimistic than his predecessors and does not expect a solution to existential problems from rational science.

Contemporary man is much less interested in rational truth than in practical efficacy. I personally do not think one superior to the other. I am happy to take men as they are, and I try to communicate with them in a language they understand. Why should I try to convince them of the Gospel with exegetical, historical, or metaphysical arguments when I already know such arguments won't convince anyone? Not that I consider these arguments useless. Once I was convinced of the existential verity of Christian revelation, I became most interested in a scientific knowledge of Christianity. But preaching the Gospel doesn't begin with that kind of knowledge.

The most serious objection to Christianity today asserts that its adherents are humanly insensitive and have no real love for the world. Such critics do not believe that Christians have truly entered into the temporal and the human and even consider them inferior. Christians, they agree, participate in scientific research and work for social progress from time to time, but they put no real trust in these values and engage in them merely to "prove that believers can do this sort of thing if they want to. Or else they use these temporal activities as a pretext for apologetic arguments. Rightly or wrongly, Christians strike those who are really interested in the world and humanity as false brothers and traitors.

We must admit that such a conception of the Christian's attitude toward the world is no mere calumnious invention of the enemies of Christianity. In fact many Christians seem to say by their behavior that their faith requires them to have contempt for the world and the human. The example of the priest-worker movement is a case in point. In the beginning, the Christian world was sympathetic toward it and even proud of such a bold initiative. This positive attitude was motivated by the hope that these young priests would minimize the dangerous Marxist influence and establish a saner social order. All the better if the workers became good Christians! But what a different reaction when it was discovered that the priest-workers had a quite different conception of their mission. They did not intend to give the appearance of belonging to the working class. They wanted to become workers in spirit and in fact. They did not subject themselves only to the sociological and economic conditions of the proletariat, but tried to share their feelings, their ideology, and their hopes.

Teilhard de Chardin's attitude toward the scientific world was analogous to that of the priest-workers toward the world of labor. In my opinion, this is the only attitude that is likely to make Christianity relevant today. Either Christians become authentic children of Mother Earth, or she will reject them as intruders. It is not enough to pretend an interest in the world, for modern man spurns such superficiality. We must become faithful children of Mother Earth in body and soul. Indeed, we should become so much more than others for we know that we are building the Kingdom of Heaven as well as an earthly society. We cannot afford the luxury of false humility. The more we become aware of the harm done to the cause of the evangelization by a certain kind of "Christian humility," the louder we ought to shout: "Brothers, be less humble and much more proud of being the collaborators of God."

In a talk to a group of Christians recently, I told them this. It made them uneasy, and they protested that I professed an "activist faith." This in their minds was a degradation of the true faith that can blossom only in contemplation of eternal truths. I must admit that this attitude, which is still that of many Christians, is absolutely foreign to me. I think religion should be active; otherwise, Christian presence in the world would make no sense. God created the world because He is Love, and since there is no change in Him, He continues to love the world. He made men his co-creators. This means that we, too, should love the world, for only he who loves is capable of acting creatively. The Apostle James is not the mystic John was. But what he wrote about our obligation to act is in keeping with the demands of Revelation as well as those of common sense.

4

You Are Strangers in the World

In a beautiful passage of *The Divine Milieu,* Teilhard de Chardin discusses with great intellectual honesty, the ambigious situation of the Christian in the world. Every Christian knows that life in this world is not an end in itself, that it finds its fulfillment in a greater life. Thus, it is not surprising that the believer takes earthly life to be of little worth, so much so that he may see in it no more than a vain agitation. From here it is only a step to condemning this world, a step that many sects and believers take only too easily. Christian perfection consists in detachment from all that is earthly.

Let us put ourselves in the place of someone who has little knowledge of Christianity. Being curious, he tries to find out what "is real" in the Christian faith. So he goes into a Church while Mass is being celebrated. He begins by observing the congregation. Everyone is so serious, indeed sad, though it is not necessarily a Mass of the Dead. He then listens to the sermon. The priest is probably talking about heaven. Our visitor learns all sorts of interesting things about a fascinating country that is far, far away—perhaps on another planet. It is a kingdom—or the republic—of souls, for the inhabitants of this marvelous world are evidently without bodies, the origin and symbol of all the miseries of the human condition; nor do they have bodily needs or passions. At this point our friend asks a question: "How do these blessed people occupy themselves?" Immediately an answer is forthcoming: The elect contemplate the Holy Virgin and the other saints and sing hymns in praise of God. Then he gets a foretaste of what this might be like as the congregation begins to sing. Something, perhaps, like *Ave Maris Stella* or *We Have But One Soul To Save.* How convinced is a stranger likely to be by all of this? He is much more likely to get the impression that Christianity condemns men to eternal boredom.

Or our friend might chance upon a Sunday sermon about life in this world. He would then learn that the earth, which he had until now found so beautiful, was nothing but a valley of tears, a land of exiles. Because of original sin, which our first parents presumably committed in the darkest night of time, all men are condemned. There is a possibility of redemption, but only on condition that one remains detached from the goods and beauties of the world, for they are false goods and deceitful beauties. They were not created for the pleasure and joy of men, but to tempt them and thus test their fidelity to God. Because of the results of original sin, man instinctively tends toward evil. Only the wicked fully enjoy the goods and beauties of this world; but in doing so, they risk eternal damnation. Other men must use them moderately. In this way, they will not be damned, but they will have to undergo the purifying flames of purgatory after death. True Christians will conduct themselves as strangers in the world, remembering always that they are on pilgrimage. They will use the goods of the earth as a means of bare subsistence, wishing they could dispense with them altogether. How enviable are those saints who can by God's grace live without any food at all. In any case, the good Christian should never become attached to the things of this world. At all times, he must be guided by humility and never aspire to the first ranks of social life. [Only the middle way, the *aurea mediocritas,* is becoming to the children of God.] The preacher would then support this point of view with examples from the lives of the saints—stirring passages of kings and popes who renounced their rank out of humility, of wise men who preferred out of love of God to appear stupid, indeed foolish, in the eyes of men.

The first question that would occur to our visitor would probably be: "How can such a man, obviously well fed and seemingly living in relatively comfortable circumstances, talk that way?" He might also observe that few people are more vain or ambitious in the worst sense of the word than certain priests, that pomp and circumstances are nowhere more ostentatiously practiced than in ecclesiastical circles. I remember being reprimanded by a very respectable archbishop because I had greeted a Protestant minister in the audience first. Examples of this kind abound.

The practical result of this hostility to the world is the present abyss between Christianity and the world. Paradoxically, the abyss is deepest in traditionally Catholic countries. It is not by pure accident that Protestant countries are generally more economically advanced than Catholic countries. And even in such countries as Belgium, France, Italy, and Spain, the economic leaders have been almost exclusively Jews, Protestants, Free Masons, or other anti-clerics. There have been very few eminent Catholic economists. Catholics who are faithful to the Church have no real interest in the affairs of the world.

This being the case, there is no place for a Christian humanism. Indeed, the word "humanism" was for centuries synonymous with anti-Christian. It was in the name of humanism that artists, writers, philosophers, and politicians since the time of the Renaissance broke with the Catholic tradition. Likewise, it was in the name of humanism that the philosophers of the eighteenth-century Enlightenment and the sociologists of the nineteenth-century reacted against Christianity. If I am not mistaken, Jacques Maritain, in his *True Humanism* (1935), was the first to revindicate the rights and necessity of a new humanism of Christian inspiration.

Happily, this hostility to the world as we have described it has nothing to do with the essence of Christianity. The terrestrial and the natural are the work of God and the object of His love. As we shall see in subsequent chapters, it is only by realizing our natural destiny as men in the world and in time that we can realize our supernatural vocation as sons of God.

5

Humanitarian Pantheisms

Karl Jaspers has said that a man who believes in nothing has not really lived, even though he should sacrifice his life. There seems to be little doubt that the need for an absolute, for something greater and more important than oneself, is one of the fundamental needs of human nature. The religious mentality has always put itself in the service of such an absolute. Experience proves that our times are no less religious in this respect than former ages. However, men today are partial to "religions" that have neither Revelation nor God. With the exception of Marxism these religions eschew dogmatism. They are able, however, to give their adherents the indispensable absolute ideal that lifts their existence above daily banalities and often inspires heroism and total sacrifice of self. Teilhard de Chardin called them "humanitarian pantheisms."

I am aware that most theologians find such an extension of the concept of religion abusive. They are right to the extent that those who adhere to what we have designated humanitarian pantheisms are frequently hostile to faith and religion. As professional theologians they are convinced that the principal characteristic of all religion is belief in God and Revelation. Since they do not believe in any God and their convictions are not founded on any Revelation, they are naturally opposed to being called "religious." I have often seen Marxists bristle with anger when they were told that their convictions were like those of religion and their party organized like a Church. And objectively they were no doubt right.

But we are not adopting an objective point of view. We are speaking psychologically. The adhesion of humanitarian pantheists to what they call "the Truth" has none of the qualifications or restrictions that are characteristic of an opinion or a scientific belief. They are convinced that they possess absolute truth, and the best of them are ready to give their life for the defense and the triumph of this truth. That not everyone recognizes this absolute for what it is changes nothing; psychologically speaking, a "subjective absolute" fulfills exactly the same function as absolute truth does for those who believe in a revealed religion.

Those whose God is their belly, as St. Paul says, cannot be counted among the humanitarian pantheists. The absolutizing of pleasure stems from a clearly narcissistic mentality and cannot be considered religious, even in the broad sense of that word. The minimal meaning attaching to the words "religion" and "absolute" transcends individual narcissism. In this sense, Jaspers says that there can be no authentic existence without transcendence. Egotistical narcissism can scarcely be considered a form of authentic existence.

There are many forms of humanitarian pantheism. But they all have this in common: namely, faith in *universal progress*. Some firmly believe in scientific progress and expect of it the liquidation of all misery, indeed all imperfection in the world. Others stress social progress and dream of an age when all men will love one another as brothers, when ignorance and poverty, intellectual and material imperfections will be abolished, when all children will be born in perfect health and generously endowed by nature. But it should be pointed out that these worshipers of progress do not content themselves with hope alone. They are not lacking in the third "theological virtue" of love. It is well-known that many scholars have consecrated their whole lives in the service of science. I have known many whose fidelity has been nothing short of heroic. There was the recent case of a doctor who performed very dangerous experiments on himself in the interests of medical science. Even though his initiative eventually led to a painful death, he was convinced that he had done something great with his life. In the theological meaning of the word, this doctor was an atheist. But his behavior was authentically religious. The humanity for which he freely underwent pain and death was an absolute for him and his individual life but a small part of the whole. Of course, not all scientists are so heroic. But then neither are all Christians in a class with a Francis of Assisi or a Charles de Foucauld. The point is that many men today strive to give their lives meaning and fulfillment by devoting themselves to scientific progress for the good of mankind.

When I was about fourteen years old I knew I could never be satisfied with the boredom of daily life. I did not only want to live; I wanted to make something great of my life. I was more or less dimly aware that I was not a product of mere biological chance, that I had some determined mission to accomplish in life. I dreamed of making geographical or scientific discoveries. But beyond this, I was in search of personal fulfillment. And I already realized that personal fulfillment could be authentic only on condition that I dedicated my life to some absolute.

One day I happened to read Maxim Gorki's celebrated novel *The Mother*. It came as a real revelation to me. There was now no room for doubt: I had to dedicate my life to the cause of exploited and oppressed humanity. At this stage, this impulse was still an abstract ideal. But the die was cast. Shortly thereafter, I joined the Communist Party, and for almost ten years worked to realize a classless society.

Of course, I considered myself an atheist. I neither believed in God nor revelation. The only source of valid knowledge I accepted was science. I was interested only in what concerned the fate of humanity. It seemed to me that to attribute the creation of man to some supreme being would be an insult to him. Hadn't Marx written: "Man must become the supreme being for man?" If I had been told then that my enthusiasm for communism had a religious or mystical character I would have been greatly surprised.

However, from a psychological point of view, my devotion to the cause of communism was quite religious. To be sure, I had no interest in the salvation of my soul since I categorically denied the existence of a soul. Words like "proletariat," "humanity," and "revolution"—which I took to be purely empirical expressions— were in fact colored with mystical overtones in my psyche. I knew that proletariats were far from perfect; many of them were very mediocre men. Yet I considered them, as a collective entity, the repository of all the virtues and all the promises of history. Moreover, communist theory taught that there would be a period of poverty and slavery before the advent of the classless society of tomorrow. "Proletariat" and "humanity" were words that took on a transcendent, quasi-Platonic meaning for me.

When I was under the death sentence in Nazi prison camps, I was young, enjoyed perfect health, and was passionately in love with life. I had no fear of death. It seemed quite logical for me to sacrifice my life for the proletariat. In my autobiography *From Karl Marx to Jesus Christ,* I wrote:

> I could only with difficulty conceive of my proximate death. From a rational point of view it only meant the end of a life that had, to be sure, been short but very intense. I found it impossible to imagine that it would serve no purpose, that everything would be reduced to nothingness. A voice that was not very orthodoxically Marxist, whispered that my death itself would serve the Cause for which I had lived, that my blood would in the end be fecund. Just how this could be, Marxist dialectic was unable to explain.

Quite wrongly, many readers of the above lines concluded that I was already implicitly professing a faith in the immortality of the soul. In fact, I am quite certain that my revolutionary optimism had absolutely nothing in common with hope in personal immortality. Of course, the irrational played a very important role in my firm belief in the solidarity of all mankind, a solidarity that embraced all time and space. I would have been quite at a loss to justify this rationally. I was equally convinced that all my actions, even the most private of them, would have some repercussion on the actions and decisions of other men. I knew that other communists shared these sentiments; but we were not for that reason "believers in spite of ourselves." We neither believed in God nor in personal immortality. We were naturalistic pantheists. The qualification "naturalistic" is an important one, for as I have said, the divine was radically excluded for our mentality. If I were not concerned with fidelity to Teilhard's terminology, I would substitute the term "pancosmism" for "pantheism." For in fact I was keenly aware of belonging to the universe, and I was little interested in what might happen to me as an individual. To contribute to the promotion of general progress was a sufficient reason for living.

I was personally interested in social progress. But I was also interested in such things as scientific progress. This, I then believed, would necessarily improve the general condition of mankind.

Gradually I came to know the limits and inadequacies of "humanitarian pantheism." When I left the Communist Party I was only vaguely aware of the real reasons for my disillusionment. Like many others I thought that the Soviet leaders had betrayed "true communism." Later it became clear to me that there was no question of betrayal; of its very nature materialistic communism cannot promote an authentic humanism. Like the spirit of sociology and science in the nineteenth century, communism and other humanitarian pantheisms misunderstand the specific essence of human reality, namely the Spirit. I will always work for social and scientific progress. However, I no longer consider it merely a means of improving man's lot. Nor do I any longer see humanity as an abstraction, but as the concrete totality of the persons who make up humanity. My belief that universal evolution tends toward an increasing spiritualization and personalization of creation I owe to Teilhard de Chardin. Progress must place all of its energies at the service of this end; if it does not, it will soon become antihistorical and inevitably contradict the law of general evolution. The tragedy of many eminent men is precisely this; they are well aware of the shortcomings of humanitarian pantheism, but they can think of no suitable alternative. I am not only thinking of the many Marxists I knew, but also of such outstanding scientists as Einstein and Oppenheimer. They were quite right to consecrate their lives to research in nuclear physics. But we can understand the horror they experienced after Hiroshima and Nagasaki. They were confronted with the possibility of the destruction of the earth and of mankind, which they cherished so dearly, as a result of their own creative discoveries.

6

The Temptation from the East

Teilhard de Chardin lived in China for a long time. He also had occasion to travel and work in India, Indonesia, Manchuria, and other countries of the Far East. With the sympathetic curiosity so characteristic of him, he always tried to know men—their customs, their beliefs, the economic and political conditions of their existence. He was particularly attracted by the charm of Oriental religions, especially those of India. Their universalism and their cosmic perspective impressed him deeply. He was enthusiastic about their "sense of totality." Despite the calumnies and accusations of his enemies, Teilhard was no pantheist; but he recognized that the West, with its deep expectation of a new revelation, would naturally turn toward India.

It is a fact that increasing numbers of thinking men in Europe and America are no longer satisfied with a purely immanent humanitarian *mystique*. After the disastrous experiences of rationalism, communism, and fascism, it seems evident to many that making "man the supreme being for man" (Marx), far from promoting the evolution of the universe, has only brought catastrophes to the world. If man is to be respected as such—and not merely in his capacity as a compatriot or a comrade in the Party—it is absolutely essential that life be transcendentally grounded.

It is interesting to note that many of the spiritual elite who seek the transcendent turn away from Christianity, the traditional religion of their civilization and culture, to the Oriental religions. Many books are written on Buddhism and Hinduism, and they are widely read. Almost all the large cities of the West have study groups that make a common and systematic effort to understand the spiritual masters of the Orient. Also, the practice of yoga is becoming more and more widespread, although its respiratory advantages are frequently stressed over its spiritual content.

There is no doubt that much of this attraction for Oriental religions is motivated by snobbery. Oriental doctrines are in style at the moment, and there are those who would rather die than be caught out of step with current fads. Too, these religions attract a number of psychologically disturbed persons. Nonetheless, many are perfectly normal and sincere in their quest. Their reasons for preferring Oriental religions to Christianity are that they find Christianity too formalistic, its authentic spirituality buried behind a wall of ceremonies, rites, social and moral traditions, all kinds of obligations that are incapable of eliciting a true religious spirit. There is a certain subjective justification in this judgment. Most of them have learned about Oriental religions through the works of such masters as Gandhi, Vivekananda, and Swami Ramdas, while they most frequently learn about Christianity through the daily mediocrity of their "practicing" neighbors. The comparison is obviously unjust. All Hindus are not Gandhis, any more than all Christians are St. Johns of the Cross! A remark of Teilhard de Chardin is pertinent here: "The Hindus disappointed me," he wrote. "One would have to live in India to understand how paralyzing and stupifying the effects of a religion which accords too much importance to rites and underestimates the spiritual meaning of progress can be."

These reservations are not intended to cast aspersions on the Oriental spirituality that attracts so many of the best of our contemporaries. I myself am an admirer of the spiritual masters of the East. In my library are works by Rabindranath Tagore, Gandhi, Aurobindo, Vinoba, and Ramdas, as well as many secondary works on Hinduism and Buddhism. I have drawn much spiritual nourishment from them. I honor Gandhi as one of the greatest saints of modern times, and I think that Swami Ramdas is spiritually akin to my favorite Christian saint: St. Francis of Assisi.

I would guess that Teilhard de Chardin has given the best explanation of Western man's fascination with Oriental religions: They are more universal and cosmic than others. The sense of the whole, of a totality, which we must recognize as the core of all mysticism, is evident nowhere more than in India. Men who love the world and who realize their need for the Absolute find it difficult to resist the charm of pantheism, especially as it is taught and professed by the masters of India.

Yet I have never personally been tempted to adhere to Hinduism. I am even convinced that Westerns who seek the fulfillment of their love of the world and of humanity in Eastern religions are exposing themselves to bitter disillusionment. This is true first of all because Oriental mysticism considers matter an illusion and a burden for the soul, while we see in it an important building stone for the City of God. (Cardinal Saliège once spoke of "holy matter" and called himself a "materialist"—understood in the fullest sense of the word.) More seriously, Oriental doctrines make no place for the reality of the human person. With Teilhard, I see in the evolution toward personalization the most fundamental characteristic of the spirit; it is by becoming a person that man realizes his complex nature. I cannot see the liberation of man from the determinism that surrounds and imprisons him coming from a total renunciation of everything natural and material. Quite the contrary. I hope such liberation will come from a synthesis between the natural and the material, on the one hand, and the personal, on the other. Oriental religions establish unity by annihilating the multiple, they achieve the one at the expense of the many. I find a unity that respects and assumes the multiple quite satisfying to the mind and spirit. The God I need and seek must show Himself as the savior of all of men's creative activity and all cosmic evolution. I cannot conceive of real becoming or real creative evolution within the perspective of Oriental pantheisms, one of whose central tenets is the eternal return.

This, then, is how I would summarize my position on Oriental religions: They satisfy a real need in their cosmic universality. But they violate in too radical a way several of my unshakable convictions about the natural order. For this reason, I think they are in the final analysis deficient.

7

Why and How Am I a Christian?

Teilhard de Chardin knew the attraction of humanitarian pantheism and Oriental religions. But it was in the Catholic faith of his
childhood that he finally found his need for the Absolute totally
satisfied. It was not easy for him to do so and, as he admits in
various writings, it was not without effort that he succeeded in
remaining faithful.

I was not born into a Catholic family, nor did I attend a Jesuit
college. Until I was twenty-seven, I knew very little about Christianity. Indeed, I knew much more about the other great world religions, for I had some natural curiosity about them; but my rejection of Christianity was so total that I had no desire to study it.
Moreover, the word "believe" had no concrete meaning for me; I
only wanted *to know*. I owe my first contact with Christianity to my
reading of the early Christian communities and, later, the Gospels.
It was almost by chance that this happened. At that time, I met
some priests and lay Catholics whose progressive attitude impressed
me. Because of my reading and contacts, I was soon persuaded that
Catholicism was the religion that best fulfilled my needs and more
or less conscious aspirations.

I also had some contact with Protestant communities. Their anti-
dogmatism pleased me, but I found them lacking in many important respects. It was my impression that they had not maintained
continuity with the primitive Christian communities that I admired
so much, that they were not sufficiently universal, and that their
spirituality was too narrow and insufficiently "cosmic." (I know
that members of these communities would not admit the validity of
my criticisms; I do not set them forth as having objective validity,

but only as my personal reactions at a given moment in my spiritual evolution.) One day, I asked an eminent Catholic priest, who had written some outstanding theological books, when his Church had been founded. His answer went something like this: "Officially some 1900 years ago but in reality at the moment God created the world. Men of all races, all cultures and even all religions belong to this Church. Indeed the whole universe belongs to it. The Church is in effect Catholic, which is to say universal." He then read some passages from St. Francis' *Fioretti* and other mystical works that confirmed his own conception of the Church. At that time, Europe was a cauldron of racism, fascism, Stalinist communism, and chauvinistic patriotism. I found it quite wonderful that my Catholic friends had the courage to profess in such circumstances the most radical universality.

Of course not all Catholics understood their religion in such universal and cosmic terms. In my diary, I wrote at some length about my contentions with Catholic society and my bitter disillusionment when I recognized that for many of its adherents Catholicism was only another sect beside other sects. But I eventually became familiar enough with the essence of Christianity to be able to distinguish between the Christian world and the Church of Jesus Christ. To be sure, the Christian world with its political and social conservatism, its conventions and bigotry, its habits and other forms of narrowmindedness provokes disgust more often than admiration. More seriously, Church leaders themselves did not always distinguish clearly the Church as the Mystical Body of Christ and the so-called Christian world; they often put their spiritual authority in the service of reactionary political, social, and scientific ends and thus contributed—generally in all good faith—to reinforce an impression that has already done much harm to the cause of the Christian religion in the modern world. I am much indebted to the magnificent example of Teilhard de Chardin for not having lost the keen sense of making necessary distinctions, even in the most painful of circumstances.

Thus, as I have often pointed out, evolution represents one of the most essential elements of my *natural belief*. It would be impossible for me to deny or doubt it. The reader can readily understand my disappointment and discouragement at the Vatican's attitude toward evolution, especially after the encyclical *Humani Generis* attempted to nail it to the pillar of infamy. I was even more hurt by the practical behavior of the Roman Curia toward progressive tendencies within the Church. Catholics, including priests, were praised for promoting the policies of conservative political parties, but those who engaged in leftist efforts were suspect or even condemned. The temporal work of the clergy was tolerated and even encouraged so long as it was confined to so-called bourgeois professions, such as journalism or business. But the priests who tried to exercise their ministry in the factories were considered unworthy. While mankind today is striving to give birth to more universal economic and political structures, the Church is still hampered by her feudal traditions.

Thus, it is difficult to count the Church among the progressive forces of the modern world. Even the morality she teaches tends more to conserve traditional values than to promote a new and higher form of life. One must agree with Teilhard when he writes: "Christianity has not developed a sense of the earth but has rather let it slumber."

My critical position toward the Church has created no real religious difficulty; I have remained unshakably faithful to the Church even when I openly disagree with her generally conservative and even reactionary positions. Not that I conceive of the Church as a purely spiritual reality, as do the Protestants. As a Catholic, I am convinced of the essential identity of the Mystical Body with the visible Church. It is not always easy to distinguish between the visible Church and the Christian world. Bishops and sometimes even the popes show by their behavior that they are an integral part of the Christian world, a world that is by and large anachronistic. Yet this does not prevent them from being authentic spokesmen for the Church of Christ. I myself am part of the Christian world, even though I am critical of it. This is quite in keeping with the law of the Incarnation. The evangelical parable of wheat and the tares is instructive here. I do not simplistically consider progressive Christians as the wheat and the others as the tares. The wheat and the tares grow together within each one of us. What is important is not to let the tares smother the good grain. Those who pretend to be exempt from tares are either hypocritical or stupid.

The Christian world must not be identified with the Church of Christ, yet this Church must always be part of some such Christian world. The Church is perfect, since it is the Church of God. The world is the workshop in which the City of God is built. As long as it is not completed the world, including the Christian world, can never be perfect. Yet this should be no cause for resignation before the imperfections of the world. We have the strictest obligation to do everything we can to transform a world that is only partially Christian. We must do everything we can to cultivate the good grain until the time of harvest.

It would be a mistake to conclude from the imperfections of the Christian world that the Church is of no worth. But it would also be a mistake to see everything in the Christian world as the will of God. The Lord forbade the servants to remove the tares until the wheat had ripened; but He did not imply that they were of equal value. The two must grow together into the time of harvest. This conforms to the laws of creative evolution.

Consequently, I see no contradiction between my critical position of a given measure of a bishop or even a pope and my filial respect for them. I had great admiration for Pius XI, but I was severely critical of Pius XII. I was a strong supporter of Cardinal Suhard, but am much less enthusiastic about the policies of certain other bishops. Yet they, too, are authentic representatives of the Church of Christ. It is the law of the wheat and the tares.

I learned the essence of Christianity from the teaching of Christ himself and his most authentic disciples, the saints. By teaching, I understand words as well as actions. I am quite convinced in my mind that this teaching has little in common with a certain kind of bourgeois, conformist, bigoted, and integralist Catholicism. I do not judge the Christian religion in terms of the latter. Moreover, I suspect that neurosis, more than stupidity or perversity, is the real reason for the deformation of Christ's real teaching.

I believe that the religion of Christ is essentially personal and communitarian. The God revealed by Christ is a Father who speaks, punishes, rewards, and loves as a *person*. Even our purest concepts of God are tainted with anthropomorphism; otherwise they would be incomprehensible to men. Such concepts are not therefore literal expressions of the Divine reality; they are rich and suggestive symbols. As such, they point incontestably to God as *personal*. Because I believe that evolution tends toward increasing personalization, I am able to find in Christianity what the Oriental religions lack. The

Christian vision places immortal persons at the summit of the Universe, persons who are called to assume responsibility for their destiny and their vocation. I deliberately spoke of "immortal persons" because to speak of the immortality of the soul to men today is to encounter inevitable misunderstandings. Teilhard de Chardin expressed the mentality of such men well when he wrote in *How I Believe:* " (To attain the summits promised by Christianity) . . . I have long been under the impression that the road was cut off from the earth, that one was expected to scale the clouds. Because the value of the Spirit and the supernatural character of the Divine was exalted, one came to look upon the soul as a temporary guest in the cosmos, a prisoner of matter." Such a conception of the soul is in reality more Neo-Platonic than Christian. Thus, to avoid all misunderstanding, I prefer to speak of the person as the evolutionary synthesis in which it is impossible to distinguish the body and soul in anything but a notional sense. The person is not something static. It is essentially dynamic in character, and in this it conforms to the laws of evolutionary creation.

However important personal salvation is in Christianity, the latter cannot be called an individualistic religion. The elite of our times are convinced that only the collective, communitarian effort of men can meet the needs of life. Almost all economic and scientific achievements are more or less directly due to the collaboration of large numbers of men. In all domains the "cult of personality" is becoming less and less justified. The boundaries between nations and continents are breaking down. In such conditions a religion that is concerned only with individual salvation can only appear anachronistic to most thinking men today and will certainly evoke no deep reponse from their psyche.

It is thus more important than ever to insist that Christianity is not a religion of individual salvation. If it is true that the hymn "I Have Only One Soul to Save" is still sung in Churches, we must see this as a relic of an age gone by. Teilhard de Chardin is faithful to the most authentic Christian tradition when he speaks of the "universal Christ," for in truth the Incarnation is in its deepest essence both personal and cosmic.

The birth of Christ in Bethlehem was not a unique event that we commemorate at Christmas time. Like all the mysteries of Christianity, the Incarnation is a continuing reality in cosmic history.

However real the human person—and Christianity has fully real-ized its reality—we must also insist upon human unity. It follows that the eternal Word, in becoming flesh, not only sanctified and divinized the individual nature of the Jewish Jesus of Nazareth, but also human nature in its totality. This at least is how the Christian tradition after Paul understood the mystery of the Incarnation, and only in this perspective does the doctrine of the Mystical Body take on its full meaning.

But human nature is intimately bound up with the nature of the universe as a whole. Men are not strangers or pilgrims on the earth; we are truly at home here. Thus I believe that Christ by becoming man implicated the whole universe in the divinizing mystery of the Incarnation. In affirming this there is no risk of pantheism unless St. Paul himself was a pantheist. The latter took it for granted that all of nature groaned with man under the burden of sin and would be redeemed with him. Not only is the Christian man an "other Christ"; the whole cosmos is likewise and will become more so in the course of its evolution toward a higher degree of spiritualiza-tion. We hold with Teilhard to a "pan-Christianity" that should not be confused with pantheism, at least in the usual sense of that word.

Pan-Christianity is still in an emergent state. It is in a process of becoming like the cosmos itself, and will likely remain so for a long time. Just as in St. Paul the Mystical Body is one with Christ, so too pan-Christianity (or the total Christ) is one with the Christ of the Gospels. Pan-Christianity pertains to the domain of evolutionary creation. This means that its realization depends on all of us, for as we have already noted, the spiritual phase, the noosphere, of uni-versal evolution can only be realized with the active collaboration of men whom God has called to be his co-creators.

It follows from the foregoing that each time we make a creative contribution of whatever kind of cosmic evolution, we by the same token collaborate in the Incarnation of the total Christ in history. Thus the Christian view of the world is not so narrow as is some-times supposed. The mystery of the Incarnation precludes any form of narrowness. Through the Incarnation, matter in all of its forms, life, and spirit, the whole cosmos have been forever and irreversibly sanctified. Christianity thus acknowledges the primordial role of matter; without it there could have been no Incarnation. Consequently, it is only through the instrumentality of my insertion in the world that I can realize my personal salvation.

Whatever beauty I found in humanitarian pantheism and the cosmic religions of the Orient, I find more fully realized in Christianity. Total Christianity, pan-Christianity, promotes the collective progress of humanity without prejudice to the individual person. It also affirms cosmic unity with God without compromising the distinction between the temporal and the eternal. It seems to me that if we wish to understand Christianity in all of its depth and breadth, we must see it not as one religion among others, but as *the* perfect religion of mankind and the cosmos. The word "Catholic" must be understood in an altogether realistic sense.

8

The Mystery of the Trinity

"The trinitarian nature of God," Teilhard de Chardin wrote, "is not unrelated to our most urgent spiritual needs. It is the essential condition of God's inherent capacity to be the personal summit—and as a consequence partially independent—of a Universe that is evolving towards personalization."

From my earliest initiation into Christianity, I was both intrigued and astonished by the most basic dogma of Christianity—the Trinity. Both the Old and New Testaments are very discreet about God's intimate life. The Incarnation, The Redemption, the Divine Paternity tell us less about God than about the kind of relation He has with His creatures. But in telling us that there are three persons in the Godhead, Revelation seems to make an exception and lift the veil on God's intimate nature.

Christians are so accustomed to professing a triune God that they have some difficulty in understanding how revolutionary such a revelation was in the religious history of mankind. We would be mistaken to interpret it as a kind of syncretism between the polytheism of the Greco-Roman world and the strict monotheism of the Jews. It takes but little reflection to understand that the Trinity is one of the most complex notions ever confronted by the human intellect. This becomes clear when we observe the efforts of theologians who tried to explicate this doctrine in light of Aristotle's doctrine of being, one of whose basic tenets was the principle of identity. All rational categories, whether ancient or modern, are inadequate before the divine paradox that affirms the trinity of persons in the unity of substance. It would have been much more reasonable to attribute Divinity to the Father alone and consider the other two persons His creatures.

I first read the Gospels without prejudice and even without any knowledge of the traditional teaching of the Church. I was convinced that both the unity and the trinity of God were basic Evangelical truths. Christ, of course, was neither a theologian nor a philosopher. He was not accustomed to abstract language. More existential than Kierkegaard himself, He spoke in an eminently concrete and symbolic language. It took the subtlety of the Greeks to translate what Christ taught about the Father, Son, and the Holy Spirit into the beautiful theological hymn of the Athanasian Creed. Nonetheless, what Christ taught was so clear that the formulae of that Creed did not surprise me when I came to know them.

It is impossible to believe that the revelation of one of the principal mysteries of the Christian faith was made to satisfy our intellectual curiosity. This would be foreign to the "existentialism" of Christ. It would be without precedent in Biblical history. Christ made short shrift of those who asked for special signs from heaven and spectacular miracles. He worked miracles only out of pity for the physical and moral miseries of mankind. He had little patience with the clever distinctions of the casuists and taught nothing that was not indispensable for the salvation of men, which is to say the realization of our vocation as men, as children and cooperators of God. Are we then presumptuous in concluding that the revelation of the Trinity was also motivated by the "utilitarian," existential end of Christ's mission?

After much reflection and meditation, two Biblical facts seem to me to be the key to this mystery. First of all, the sacred writings teach us that God created man in His image and likeness. It is evident that this likeness cannot be a human one since we are much more akin to matter than to Absolute spirit. We have to do with an ideal toward which we must tend, with a task that each individual in particular and humanity as a whole must work to realize. "Be ye perfect as the heavenly Father is perfect." St. Paul indicates the path to be followed: "Be my imitators as I myself am an imitator of Christ."

It is permissible to think that Christ revealed the mystery of the Trinity as a concrete indication of the kind of likeness to God we must strive to realize. If the three Divine persons are a single God and share the whole of Divinity, is it not possible for us humans to be like God in realizing as perfect a unity and community among us as possible? Not a few eminent Christian thinkers have understood the dogma of the Trinity in this fashion.

In view of this, the disciple of Christ must reject all individualism and strive for the creation of an authentically communitarian society. As long as our thinking and behavior are individualistic and egocentric, we will existentially deny the mystery of the Trinity, however fervently we recite the Credo.

The Christian is communitarian because he believes in the Trinity. He strives toward love and universal understanding because he knows that it is only in this way that he can *actualize* the image of God in himself. He must therefore be the sworn enemy of all narrow-mindedness, all sectarianism; only on this condition can he remain bound to the Whole.

For these reasons, I think that those who claim communism is of evangelical inspiration are quite right. But this is communism insofar as it represents a rejection of all individualism and calls for a common pooling of the spiritual and material wealth of the world. Communism as it is today, with is materialism, its economic structure, its violence and practical contempt for men, obviously bears no relationship to the mystery of the Trinity. If so many are confused on this point, it is perhaps because Christians have for too long given only lip service to the dogma of the Trinity and failed to comprehend the living mystery.

9

"Eppur Si Muove"

According to Teilhard de Chardin, men today fall into two categories: Some believe, with what seems like a naïve optimism, that mankind is on the march toward a better future, despite its faults and contradictions. Others affirm that nothing really changes, that everything remains the same. Since it is impossible to work up any enthusiasm for the immobile, the pessimists are forced to skepticism and resignation. They rely on the police and other social powers to maintain the status quo.

I wouldn't want to be considered naïve, but I must admit that I have never been tempted by the immobile or the pessimistic. For a long time, I thought that only the stupid could belong to this category; later experience forced me to admit that the neurotic, who lack self-confidence, are also incapable of launching healthily into the waters of human destiny. I am aware that the physical universe about me has changed little. I have never witnessed one of those epic transformations that scientific works speak of. But my fifty years are such a short time by comparison with the history of the universe! Even the history of mankind is a small island in the ocean of millions of years of cosmic history. We know that a photograph can immobilize the man who runs, the tree that grows, and the fruit that ripens. But we would not conclude that movement, growth, and ripening are deceiving appearances.

To be precise, few educated men today deny the evolution of the physical world. Anti-evolutionists oppose only the transformation of species, less for scientific than religious reasons. They think that man would lose something of his dignity as the son of God if he were the result of a biological process.

65

Galileo's expression—*eppur si muove*—must be understood in a moral and social sense today. The whole of Christian morality is founded on the conviction that man can perfect himself and, in certain cases, achieve sanctity. According to the pessimists, such an achievement would be rigorously individual; even the children of saints would have to begin at the beginning. Freudian psychoanalysis and a certain Christian pessimism agree that man is at bottom a barbarian and there is no such thing as human progress. The same would be true of collective and social issues. The world today, for example, is not superior to the medieval world. In fact, upon close inspection it is seen to be in many ways less advanced. Consequently, all political or social progressivism is to be considered a dangerous utopia that can only lead humanity to disaster. The wisest thing we can do is conserve the existing social order.

Partisans of this position do not consider the existing order perfect. Their position toward the world is too pessimistic to permit them to see anything authentically good in it. Not believing in progress, they resign themselves to the lesser evil, which is to say immobility and conservatism. These Christians are incapable of any enthusiasm with respect to worldly realities. They reason as follows: "What exists, is neither good nor beautiful but we are at least familiar with it. We know how to deal with it and thus lessen the chances of catastrophe. The new cannot be any better than the old and moreover always involves a risk. Now nothing worthwhile can come from such risks. They must, therefore, be avoided. We are aware that the captialistic system has its faults which the Christian must recognize. He must do everything he can to offset the evils inherent in a society founded on the merciless law of supply and demand. With the approval and encouragement of the Church, fervent Christians have founded innumerable religious orders dedicated to helping orphans, the poor, the old and the sick. All Christians must contribute, with money or by action, to the charitable work of the Church. Only on this condition can the capitalist justify his fortune. The only real alternative to capitalism is the medieval system." The nostalgia for the medieval guild system has never completely disappeared from the Catholic mentality. Dollfuss in Austria, Salazar in Portugal, Franco in Spain, Pétain in France, and reactionary politicians in other countries enjoyed the sympathy of the Catholic hierarchy and many Catholic laymen precisely because they attempted to restore such an order.

Today, at least in economically advanced countries, this dream has been abandoned. Even in countries like Spain and Portugal the hierarchy is becoming less and less tolerant of reactionary regimes and sometimes enters into open conflict with them. It seems now to be generally understood that no return to the past is possible. Even the hierarchy timidly admits that industrial society may not necessarily have been the invention of the Devil. It is admitted that such a society has done much to raise the standard of living. The Catholic world is less reactionary than it was a few years ago, but it is still as conservative as ever, especially in traditionally Catholic countries. It speaks of correcting the "errors" and "abuses" of capitalism, but has never clearly confronted the necessity of replacing capitalism with a new social order.

With Teilhard de Chardin, I consider the terms "Christianity" and "conservatism" radically contradictory. I don't think I am motivated in this by my Marxist past. One of my reasons for leaving the Party was precisely because, despite progressive phraseology in the Soviet Union, it was against every form of authentic human progress and was just as conservative as capitalism in those countries it controlled. Confusion about the terms "progressive" and "communist" has certainly made even progressive Christians hide behind the mantle of conservatism. I have noticed this particularly in Germany and Switzerland; but even in France, the editor of a progressive journal denied the label out of fear of being called a fellow traveler of communism. In fact, communism is not so much anticapitalist as supercapitalist. Contrary to its claims, it has never dialectically overcome what Christians criticize in capitalism—namely, the alienation of man through an impersonal economico-political regime, the dehumanization of human relations, etc. In fact, communism has aggravated the condition of alienation. But the identification of communism with progressive tendencies is so well-established that I have great difficulty convincing my fellow Catholics that it was not out of sympathy with capitalism that I broke with communism. Quite the contrary. Because my anticapitalist stance is so uncompromising, I reject its principles and methods even when they pose under the rubric of communism. As my Christian faith matures, I am becoming more anticapitalist and anticommunist. For I believe that Christianity is by its very nature a religion of progress and renewal and as such irreconcilable with all forms of conservatism.

It seems scientifically established that both the hylosphere and the biosphere underwent gigantic revolutions in the course of their evolution; but they also exhibit continuing growth. The passage from simple to more complex forms, which has been established by the sciences of nature, is today almost universally regarded as progress. Likewise, it seems scarcely debatable that man himself constitutes the highest degree of evolution within the biosphere to date and that with his advent begins a new era in evolutionary creation, the era of the spirit, the noosphere.

The issue between "conservatives" and "progressives" is best seen with respect to man. Paradoxically, a certain Christian tradition and Freudian psychoanalysis agree in that both consider man nonperfectible. The Christian pessimists attribute the radical corruption of human nature to original sin; even the Incarnation cannot fully repair the ravages of sin. Psychoanalysis, of course, does not admit the doctrine of original sin, but attributes man's intrinsically evil nature to the unconscious.

It seems to me that the explanation of such pessimism is to be found in the *a priori* individualism both Freudians and Christians profess. Man is artificially isolated from his social, cultural, and historical environment. Such an environment is considered accidental, with no real bearing on the soul of man. This individualism is understandable in Freud who was, after all, a child of the nineteenth century. But it is less comprehensible in Christians who should know that the doctrine of the Mystical Body constitutes the essential element of Christian humanism. The individual as such is a mere abstraction, useful perhaps for speculative thinking, but of no existential value whatsoever.

Concrete man is a social creature. This is what is most specifically human in his nature. Teilhard de Chardin was of the opinion that the evolution of the universe would henceforth tend not toward the perfection of the individual, but toward realizing humanity more and more fully as a whole. If Christian morality is to accomplish its primary task, which is to promote the future of mankind, it must be more concerned with collective perfection than individual perfection. If most of the Christian thinkers of former times thought that society would be improved if individuals were better, we are more inclined today to think that individuals will be better if humanity is improved as a collective reality.

Even were we to admit with the pessimists that individual human progress is impossible, it seems scarcely contestable, when we examine the matter closely, that mankind taken collectively is much more evolved than the humanity of, say, several thousand years ago, or even a few centuries ago. Let us take an example. All of civilized humanity protested against the cruelties of Nazi concentration camps, against Stalin's systematic liquidation of his political enemies, and against the Red Army's suppression of the Hungarian people in 1956, as well as against the Algerian war and the bloody events in the Congo after it attained independence. We find it quite normal that the Christian conscience be particularly enraged by anything that goes against human dignity. Nonetheless, the adversaries of Christianity are always ready to question our sincerity by recalling the "Holy" Inquisition, the fate of John Hus, Savonarola, and Galileo and so many other eminent and innocent men who were persecuted, tortured, and killed in the name of Christ. And, as a matter of fact, the Spanish Inquisitor Torquemada is more comparable to Hitler than to Francis of Assisi. Those who reproach us thusly are right from a rigorously objective point of view.

But I do not think that Christians today can be accused of hypocrisy when they become indignant at the dishonor inflicted upon humanity, just because Christians of other ages did not exhibit similar indignation. I think there has been appreciable progress in the Christian consciousness in the past two or three centuries. I am also convinced that this progress is a direct result of the slow maturation of the evangelical grain of wheat. Even those who are anti-Christian, and attribute the evolution of the collective consciousness to anti-Christian ideologies, must admit that the Word upon which our respect and love for man and mankind is based stems directly from Christian revelation.

We have no right to forget that modern man's high awareness of his dignity as man has its roots in the Christian doctrine of the Incarnation. Modern humanism is in one sense a negation of Christianity, but it is a dialectical negation because it affirms and promotes precisely those Christian values that the Christian world neglected. "Communism is a witness to the unrealized work of Christians," Nicholai Berdyaev wrote. And Chesterton said: "Communism draws its strength from Christian ideas gone mad." What is true of communism is equally true for most of the other forms of modern, atheistic progressivism.

I do not think there can be any doubt that there has been real human progress and, consequently, that progressivism is no mere historical utopia. I am further convinced that such progress is not a betrayal of the true Christian spirit; rather it corresponds to its deepest demands. We must never forget the fundamental truth that God did not create the universe once and for all, that His creative activity will continue until the end of time, and that man is His co-creator.

We rightly regret that progress—whether moral or psychological, spiritual or social—is not realized more quickly, and that it is beset with so many errors and false starts. But both Teilhard de Chardin and Bergson held that creative evolution was subject to necessary "relapses." Intellectually, this is a satisfactory theory, but it is not very consoling emotionally. That evolution takes place slowly should in no way give us excuse to cease our efforts for progress. Quite the contrary. Human progress is not given once and for all; it is a perpetual challenge for us and must always be taken up afresh. Arguments for or against progress are based on a false problem or at least a problem that is badly formulated. We want to encompass a dynamic reality within static concepts. This can never be done. The evidence for progress seems so indisputable to us that, despite some relatively valid objections, we make bold to appropriate Galileo's celebrated saying: *Eppur si muove!*

10

Aspirations Toward Unity

In the preceding chapter, we concluded that there is real progress in the universe and that henceforth this progress will be realized chiefly along the lines of self-awareness and spiritualization. Whatever the failures attendant upon this evolution, the march forward will continue. Nor will it take place mechanically; it requires our active and free collaboration. But what form should our action take? Teilhard de Chardin answered this important question in *The Future of Man:* "If we wish to safeguard the pre-eminence of the Spirit we must pursue the only path that remains open to further developments of consciousness—the path of unification." This is not an easy way, for the centripetal and egocentric forces are strong in each of us. We shall have to renounce many things that seem specifically "ourselves," but, as Teilhard says, this is the only way "to safeguard the dignity and hopes of being."

It is not impossible, although not proved, that Freudian analysis is right in affirming that there is no essential difference between the instincts and unconscious impulses of educated Western man today and those of some African tribesman or the scarcely human primitives who inhabited the earth 100,000 years ago. But we should not forget the truth that such instincts and impulses are far from being what is specifically human in man. The conscious self, the fruit of culture and civilization, is not a more or less accidental superfluity, but is at least as constitutive of our humanity as the unconscious. It is possible that if a child of a highly cultivated European family grew up with a primitive tribe he could become a savage. On the other hand, it is unlikely that a savage brought up in a civilized family would lose all of his primitive traits. Individual evolution must have attained a certain degree of maturity before man can become part of the collective progress of a given civilization.

It is almost certain that until now the spiritual evolution of humanity has been realized principally in the sense of heightened self-awareness and personalization. This progress can hardly be credited to fate or mechanical causality. Men have contributed to their own becoming, and there is no reason to think that they could not have given the spiritual progress of the universe an appreciably different direction. Nor is there any reason why this progress shouldn't continue. We have no justification for thinking that humanity has attained the highest realization of its potential and that in the future it can only destroy itself or regress. I am in agreement with Teilhard de Chardin who thought that, far from being at the summit of spiritual progress, we are on the contrary in the middle of one of its first phases. There is no doubt that future progress will be beset with as many dangers and risks as past progress. History teaches us that our ancestors did not always choose the most direct road of evolution. We have only to think of what, theoretically, should have been the spiritual evolution of the world since Christ brought his message of love and peace. But there were the atrocities of the Crusades, the Inquisition, religious wars, and the contemporary triumph of atheism and materialism. Our present control over natural forces increases our chances for new spiritual progress, but it also multiplies the risks of catastrophe and self-destruction.

There is much talk today about the meaning of history. Historical materialism takes this meaning to be the construction of communist society. Humanity, whether it wills it or not, is on the march toward communism. The only liberty it has is to hasten or retard this inevitable evolution. It also enjoys a certain liberty with respect to the means and methods to be used in the construction of this new form of society. No Marxist has any doubt that communism alone is capable of leading mankind to the highest summits of progress.

I don't think it is possible to take this narrow form of historical fatalism seriously. The Marxist schema of social evolution is not the result of a scientific observation of the facts—the convergent tendencies of past evolution, for example. It is a mere *a priori* fiction, an *ideology*. To maintain their thesis, invented to serve the needs of the cause, Marx, Engels, and their first followers were obliged to arbitrarily simplify the past history of social evolution. In fact, evolution has in no place been realized so directly as to permit us to predict its future course with certainty. Bergson was quite right: The laws of causality are more evident after than before the event. We must also reckon with the relapses of creative evolution. These relapses can on occasion be important enough to give a whole new direction to evolution. Above all, we must not forget man himself and his role in working for the advent of the noosphere. As we have pointed out, this role will be far more important in the future than it has been in the past, for we are today much more able to consciously promote historical progress than were our ancestors of only two or three generations ago. It is possible that the society of tomorrow will be communistic, but only on condition that men want it that way.

However, not everything depends on our collective convenience. There is a certan meaning of history we must take into account if we wish to build something constructive. No one can predict the future. What the world will be like in the year 3000 is a matter of general conjecture.

There are no metaphysical grounds for predicting with certitude the path of historical becoming. But because of geology, biology, paleontology, prehistory, sociology, psychology, and other exact sciences, we are now in a position to pass judgment on a relatively vast area of cosmic evolution. Consequently, we have some scientific justification to comment upon certain fundamental tendencies. With the reservation that no catastrophe intervenes to nullify our probable estimates, we can suppose, and this on good scientific grounds, that future evolution will resemble the past in all essential respects.

In observing the past evolution of the universe, we note that the existing energies—first of all in the hylosphere, then in the biosphere—always tend toward a more perfect structuralization. This goal—and here we have every right to speak of the finality of evolution—is not always attained. Many evolutionary starts abort. But this does not change the fact that progress in general is always realized in the same way. Can we expect still further progress in the hylosphere and biosphere? It would seem so. It is possible that such progress, which will result in new forms of matter and life, is already taking place in nature. Our descendants some thousands of years from now will be able to assess the results of this progress. But in all likelihood this hypothetical progress will be realized according to the general law of evolution. But whatever the future modifications of the structure of matter and life, we believe with Teilhard de Chardin that the most important theater of evolution will henceforth be the noosphere.

As in the past, the evolution of the noosphere will be essentially realized on the social plane. It goes without saying that individuals will continue to progress in the future; the personal being of today is certainly more mature than that of yesterday, and that of tomorrow will be physically superior to what it is today. Yet the progress we anticipate (for there will certainly be progress and in no case regression) will be primarily in the form of the growth of humanity as a whole. The individual, without losing the awareness of his own personality, will be more conscious of his appurtenance to the Whole.

Thus the realization of humanity as a whole is now the principal task of noospheric evolution. From the beginning, human existence has always been an organic reality, which is to say socially structured. But until now there have been only "closed" societies—clan, tribe, nation—the word "closed" being understood in its Bergsonian sense. Although certain wise men of the past envisaged universal human unity and proposed concrete means to this end, the most real awareness of human unity stems from Christian revelation, particularly the doctrine of the Mystical Body. Against the revelation of this doctrine the division of humanity and conflicting nationalisms can only appear scandalous. In recent years, there has been renewed theological interest in this doctrine. And only in the past thirty years have Christians begun to take seriously the fundamental unity of the children of God.

But reactionary and centrifugal tendencies are still in evidence. As in all great turning points of history, the partisans of immobilism or a return to the past are particularly active. Nationalism, sectarianism, racism, and even certain forms of primitive social organization find zealous supporters today. But the nationalistic terminology still used by some politicians is totally anachronistic today. It is ridiculous and embarrassing to hear reactionary politicians trying to arouse an audience with harangues about the glories of the motherland. Most people today are aware that such nationalism is an outdated myth and corresponds to nothing in reality. Man's basic predilection for the corner of the earth in which he was born and lives is, of course, a healthy instinct, provided it forms part of his general love for mankind. For the unity to which men aspire today has nothing to do with uniformity or the abolition of plurality.

The survival of nationalism is not the only obstacle to human unification. Class consciousness, formerly so vaunted, is also becoming outdated. Of course, we readily grant that class consciousness among the workers played a very positive historic role in the nineteenth century, and we are indebted to it for much progress in social justice. Nor would we wish the proletariat to renounce his class consciousness only to be exploited by another class. Quite the contrary. All class domination seems to have reached a degree of perfection sufficient to enable each group and each person to administer justice by means other than war, even though these new means may at first prove difficult in practice.

Is such a vision of human unity utopian? I would like to remind the "realists" that frequently in history the so-called utopians saw clearly and were right. But we are concerned here with something much more important than a simple scholastic quarrel between pessimists and optimists, realists and utopians. The very future of humanity is at stake. If men today are unable to surmount the divisions between tribes, nations, and classes, they run the risk of terrible catastrophes that would imperil not only the well being of mankind, but its very survival. Hopes for human unity are not utopian; what is utopian is the hope that disarmament treaties and international controls will be enough to protect us from nuclear war. Either we make every effort to create a "United States of the World" or very soon there will be neither states nor men left upon the face of the earth.

The present level of consciousness and control over nature is sufficiently high to guarantee the success of liberty over fatality and progress over catastrophe. Nothing more grandiose or more terrible can be imagined than that henceforth the destiny of mankind depends to a large extent on men themselves. The choice is not between conservatism or liberalism, but between evolutionary progress and a catastrophe that would victimize all of humanity.

Clearly there can be no turning our backs on progress. But since this progress requires psychological preparation and the collective efforts of humanity one and indivisible, a new and very important question must be asked: Will this future unified humanity be obliged, in virtue of some historical determinism, to take on a given structure, or will it be free to invent forms of social life of its own choice?

We know the Marxist communist's answer. According to him, history follows the laws of strict determinism. Everything bears a causal relationship to the conditions of production. To understand this concept it is well to recall the physics of the nineteenth century —considered by educated men to be the model of all scientific disciplines. In order to adapt sociological conditions to the physics of their time, Marx and his followers fell back upon an excessive simplification of history. The old "feudalism" was supposedly dialectically denied or "liquidated" by capitalism. By means of an abusive application of Hegel's dialectic to the sociological order, Marxism then interpreted feudalism as the "thesis" and capitalism as the "antithesis." Communism was to effect the "synthesis." Marx's theory seemed strikingly evident to many of his contemporaries. Thus the poet Heine was terrified by the thought that the communist future would bring the uneducated masses to power. This could only lead to the denigration, if not the total destruction, of all higher cultural values. But a reading of Marx convinced him that this state of affairs was inevitable and that he had no alternative but to resign himself to it.

Today, it is easy enough to see the weaknesses in Marx's philosophy of history. We know for example that there were other forms of autonomous social organization besides feudalism before capitalism. Furthermore, capitalism itself underwent considerable evolution, so much so that its absorption by communism seems less and less inevitable. Modern physics, for its part, has completely abandoned its mechanistic presuppositions; consequently, materialism has lost much of its vaunted scientific foundation. It is also philosophically evident that the terms "dialectic" and "materialist" are radically irreconcilable.

But our real problem is not the historical and philosophical refutation of Marxist sociological determinism. Material elements are very important; but we must never forget that evolution can be realized only with the free collaboration of men. It would seem that the objective factors influencing social development today are more numerous and more powerful than formerly. Together with these objective factors there has been a gigantic increase of human liberty. If men wish to orient their future toward communism it would be very possible for them to do so, at least for what concerns the immediate future. But there are other possibilities as well. Thus the real question before us today is: Since we are convinced that life is purposeful—and not deterministic—and human evolution has direction, should we consider communism one of its stages, provisory to be sure, but nonetheless important and desirable? If the answer to this question is affirmative, then we have a duty to collaborate with communism in striving to humanize it from within.

A good number of Christians are convinced that communism is in its reality a progressive movement and therefore of great historical importance. They find some confirmation of their point of view in Teilhard de Chardin who also thought that mankind's only chance of avoiding anarchy was in the "socialization" of human coexistence.

Teilhard was convinced that human evolution tends principally toward the fulfillment of humanity as a whole. To be more precise: He thought that individual perfection would in the future be in terms of the realization of the potential of total humanity. But Teilhard's perspective does not suppose the abolition or even the diminution of the *personal* role of men in society; nor does it suppose the dissolution of the person in some pantheistic divinization after death. As we hope to show in a later chapter, eternal salvation, although communitarian in its essence, can only be conceived of as a fulfillment of all the personal qualities of men. Since we view all temporal progress, in the final analysis, as a preparation for eternal life, we cannot consider really progressive an ideology or a social regime that is not expicitly concerned with the promotion of personal reality, whatever social transformations they may otherwise effect.

If communism were a mere ideology, its capacity to promote or abase the human person could be discussed philosophically. But in our time communism is a concrete historical and sociological reality. I myself labored six years in its ranks for the "liberation of humanity." I felt obliged in conscience to break with it because it became clear to me that communism tended to enslave men spiritually rather than inspire them to higher forms of existence. The materialism of communism is neither historical nor dialectical, but expressly metaphysical. And it seems to me that this metaphysical

materialism is so essential to communism that it could never renounce it without renouncing its very nature. Since the progress of
humanity must be realized in terms of greater personalization and
spiritualization, we are forced to conclude that communistic Marxism is not in step with history. Consequently, its claim to be an
ideology and a progressive movement can only be taken seriously by
the intellectually confused.

Increasing socialization signals the veritable beginning of the era
of the person. But the envisaged unity must not be identified with
the uniformity of some totalitarian state. The social body that
mankind is in the process of building is a highly differentiated and
living body. No organ loses its proper value because it functions in
view of the life and growth of the whole body. An ideally socialized
humanity would have as its model the doctrine of the Mystical
Body as defined by St. Paul, although the distinction between the
temporal and the eternal would have to be maintained. Love would
be the animating force of all parts of the body. It seems to me that
this is the sense in which John XXIII spoke of socialization. Those
who interpret his remarks as an effort to reconcile Catholicism and
communism are wrong. History is moving toward a community and
not a collectivity.

Is it utopian for Christians to expect more from the dialectic of
love than the dialectic of class struggle? We admit that at the
present stage of evolution love has not played an important role in
the formation of societies. As Bergson pointed out in his *Two
Sources of Religion and Morality,* men in the past organized almost
uniquely against other groups: tribe against tribe, confederation
against confederation, state against state. All such groups were
"closed" societies. They constituted a necessary step in human evolution, but it would be a mistake to consider them the only way in
which society can be organized. It is our opinion that closed societies have become as anachronistic as wooden plows and horse-
drawn carriages.

All Christians should welcome and encourage the efforts to
abolish national frontiers and class warfare. They should also recognize that they are not capable of creating the new world, the open
society of the future, alone. Even if they were to create a new
Christianity, fundamentally different from medieval Christianity, it
would not be a truly open society. The modern world is in fact
pluralistic. Men of very different beliefs and convictions inhabit it

and collaborate together. The progress of the noosphere cannot be aided by erecting barriers between different spiritual families. The historical task with which we are charged demands the conjoined efforts of all men of good will, and this good will is not the exclusive privilege of any Church.

During the Second World War, Teilhard de Chardin recommended a new "order of knights" composed of men who recognized that the evolution of the universe had reached a decisive, new turning point. These men—Christians, non-Christians, and unbelievers—seemed to him to constitute a "homogeneous category." He knew from personal experience that such men, animated by a living faith in the future of humanity, were capable of a kind of love and cooperation that transcended all rational and confessional boundaries. This capacity for love must be put in the service of the great historical task that is the creation of a world society. Such an idea is not as utopian as it might seem. We can see something of the shape of the new society by comparing Europe today with the collection of antagonistic nations it long was. I consider the Franco-German alliance a particularly important step.

Let us insist once again that our conception of socialization, which we share with Teilhard and Pope John, is not to be identified with statism, whether of the capitalistic or communistic variety. It is clear that private possession of the means of production, as conceived and realized by classical capitalism, no longer corresponds to the needs of human evolution. It has proved unable to promote the common good and social peace. It is a relic of the age of individualism that has gone forever. Neither the domination of one people by another—colonialism—nor the domination of one class by another—capitalism—corresponds to the present level of human consciousness, whether individual or collective. Anachronistic attachment to capitalist private property, so long dear to Christians, in the final analysis benefited only materialistic communism, just as the obstinate efforts of so many to preserve colonialism aided communist efforts. Yet we have been taught for two thousand years that we must not put new wine in old bottles.

The time has come to definitely break with all the old categories and admit the capitalism, communism, liberalism, fascism, and most of the other "isms" are all equally reactionary. We must create something entirely new.

11

The Sacrament of Love

"From a realistic point of view," Teilhard de Chardin writes in his *Introduction to the Christian Life,* "the sacraments are not only symbolic rites. They operate biologically because they represent a life of personal union with God. This idea of the organic function of a sacrament is nowhere more apparent than in the Eucharist." This is the most "catholic," which is to say the most universal, of all the sacraments. In almost all religions, under different forms, there are rites and ceremonies intended to enable man to assimilate himself to the divine, which is usually done by means of eating. I have always found it strange that certain historians of religion, as well as would-be intellectuals who read them too uncritically, have been able to draw from the fact of the universality of the rites and symbols of communion arguments against the Christian doctrine of the Real Presence. I see in it one of the fundamental spiritual aspirations of man.

I believe that Christ is *really* present in the Eucharist, that by one of these wonders of love whose secret God alone knows, men are ordained to render Christ sacramentally present under the species of bread and wine.

How are we to conceive of this sacramental presence? Believers have always asked this question. If it is in fact true that faith is not merely an affair of the intelligence, it nonetheless seeks understanding. *Fides quaerens intellectum,* as St. Augustine put it.

The attentive reader of the Gospel account can scarcely deny the realism of this sacrament. To be sure, we have to do here with a symbol. But we must not forget that only after the truimph of post-Cartesian materialistic rationalism did the dichotomy between symbol and reality, symbolism and realism, set in. In the Judeo-Christian tradition, as in the spiritual traditions of Greece, India, and other civilizations, it was always understood that a symbolic action signified *more* than the material signs and gestures by which it was effected, which is to say it is more real than the signs and gestures themselves.

Today, the theories that theologians elaborated within the framework of Aristotelian physics cannot satisfy the legitimate intellectual curiosity of either believers or unbelievers. Conceiving matter to be a solid and opaque substance, these theologians were forced to perilous intellectual acrobatics to explain how one substance could be replaced by another. We know in the light of modern physics that matter is far from being an opaque and solid substance. It is essentially an energy always in movement and is just as difficult to understand as the "substantial form" of the ancients. Today the dogma that affirms that the bread and the wine really become the body and blood of Christ is much less offensive to our reason because it is easier for us to go from the quantitative to the qualitative order.

From the metaphysical point of view, the body and blood of Christ we receive sacramentally is identical with the body and blood of Jesus of Nazareth who was born of Mary and crucified under Pontius Pilate. But this is not the case from a phenomenological point of view. The body of the Resurrected Christ, glorious in a nonspatial heaven, must evidently be a *spiritual body,* and it is this body that is present in the Eucharist. This is far from the popular view of the Real Presence. Some naïve persons still refuse to bite the host because they think it will make Christ bleed. But the new Testament teaching on the Eucharist is in perfect accord with the view we are expounding here. Modern scientific theories of matter clarify the mystery of transubstantiation much better than the old physics of material substances.

The body, like all matter, is by its very nature a unit of energy. Therefore, we must think of Christ's sacramental presence *energetically.* The concept of energy is just as real as symbolic concepts. Isn't there more reality in movement than in stagnation, in action than in passivity? The resurrected and glorious Christ can only be actively present in the Eucharist. Pious metaphors such as "prisoner of the tabernacle" are radically irreconcilable with the condition of Christ's glorious body present in the Eucharist. Christ does not become bread and wine; rather bread and wine become His body and blood. Christ is not imprisoned in the Eucharistic species; rather these species are spiritualized and liberated from the limitations of matter.

In conformity with authentic Christian teaching, we see in Eucharistic communion not so much a means of individual sanctification, but the very efficacious cement of the Christian community. Because we communicate sacramentally, we share in Christ's own divinity. We gradually become part of a Christo-genesis, says Teilhard, which is but the soul of a universal Cosmo-genesis. Because we all communicate in the same mystery, we are united by divine bonds. Eucharistic communion is the basis of a specifically Christian human fraternity.

12

Faith in the Peace of the World

A man as convinced as Teilhard de Chardin of the fundamental unity of the human race and one who worked so hard to effect this unity would obviously have to take sides on the agonizing question of war and peace. "Nothing is more dangerous for the future of the world," he wrote in *The Future of Man*, "and indeed nothing less founded on nature than that resignation and false realism with which many people, heads lowered and shoulders hunched, predict (and thereby provoke) a new cataclysm for tomorrow."

No depth psychologist can doubt that the fear and panic before the possibility of a new war, which would certainly be much more terrible than all the wars of the past, are the principal causes of moral disorder that plagues the contemporary world. Most men are probably not aware of this reason for their despair; indeed, they might not even realize that they are in despair. But when we begin to probe into the unconscious motives of practical behavior we soon discover, especially in the young, the paralyzing effect of fear of war. Teilhard de Chardin pointed this out, with his customary prophetic clairvoyance, as early as 1947 long before the cold war and armaments race. Among my patients in psychotherapy are a number of young men, many of them highly talented, who show no interest in their studies or any other form of preparation for adult responsibilities. Their parents accuse them of laziness. But this is far too superficial a diagnosis. The psychologist knows from experience that laziness is more often a symptom than a cause. In many of these cases it is clear that psychic insecurity, largely motivated by fear of war, is the real cause of their laziness and lack of faith in the future. Even those who are not consciously aware of this have somehow the impression that it is pointless to put such effort into acquiring a degree when the future is so uncertain and the possibility of a nuclear war so great. Since this is the case, why not enjoy life as much as possible? Many adults would be surprised to learn how much anxiety and despair the therapist uncovers in these young people who seem merely superficial and selfish. Their gaiety is usually a front; they in fact find little joy in their amusements. They have often told me that their capers are a way of distracting themselves from the unpleasant prospects of the future, that in reality they are bored, that neither sex nor alcohol really calms their fears. How different from my own youth! After the First World War, both young and old were pretty well-convinced that the horrors they had so recently witnessed would never be repeated, that never again would men take arms against one another. Some, and I was among them, put their hopes in communism whose proximate triumph in the world would promote universal fraternity. Others expected much from the United Nations and international police forces. Today, I don't know anyone who places any faith in international organizations such as the United Nations or disarmament conferences. The communists are still able to capture the enthusiasm of youth; but it is becoming increasingly difficult for them to attract dedicated militants. Even faithful members of the Party have lost faith in the future. They are as skeptical about a classless society as the Christian is about a terrestrial paradise in which the lion and the lamb will lie down together.

I have learned from experience that the best way to cure the young of their "laziness" is to convince them that a thermonuclear war is by no means necessary, that the future of humanity depends above all and to a large extent on the behavior of men, that this future can become, if we so desire, much more beautiful than past ages. But the young can become convinced of this only if the example is set by adults.

I am aware, of course, of the influence, if not the validity, of arguments against our faith in the possibility of a universal and lasting peace. There are many "wise men" and "realists" who say: "Wars have always existed and always will." Or: "Man is intrinsically corrupt, and the progress of civilization and culture doesn't change this. On the contrary, we have only to consider the unparalleled atrocities of World War II." Sometimes they draw an argument from science and point out that the struggle for life is the very motor force of evolution. If this struggle should cease, there would be no further evolution, and life would stagnate. War, therefore, is not only inevitable, but necessary.

But our optimism is not dampened by such arguments, even though they are well grounded in the past experience of mankind. For we have no doubt that the history of the universe has reached an entirely new era, and for this reason, the old laws of nature are no longer valid. From a biological point of view, living species were often forced to destroy one another in the past in order to survive because the needs of all could not be satisfied. But it is clear today that technology provides us with the instrument for satisfying our needs peacefully.

There is no longer any biological need for war; the problem of war and peace is now a moral issue. It is a matter of human liberty. War will be difficult to avoid in the future, but for the reason that men are not sufficiently aware of their ontological unity. As long as the rich nations, for example, continue to dump products to keep prices high while millions starve, there is obviously no realistic hope for world peace. Today, the greatest threat to world peace is not the good or bad will of this or that statesman, but that men of all countries and all races do not adequately understand that their mutual interests are much more complementary than exclusive. The world powers can certainly come to peaceful terms. But as long as great poverty exists side by side with great wealth, the danger of war will remain.

The abolition of economic and other injustices is therefore a necessary condition for world peace. This, as the Gospel teaches, will be the work of men of good will. But it should be stressed that this good will is not the same as vague, idealistic aspirations; it is essentially a faculty of action. We are also firmly convinced that the good will we are speaking of here is in natural accord with the progress of the noosphere. We are speaking here of the good will of a human nature redeemed by Christ; the "pure" nature exalted by Jean Jacques Rousseau is a mere abstract fiction.

Great as is our optimism, we do not take world peace for granted. History teaches us that evolution is never realized without relapses and deviations. It is not only probable, but unfortunately certain that there are still today and will be tomorrow at least restricted wars. Nor is a devastating world war a philosophical or psychological impossibility. Our only argument is that it is not necessary; it can be averted. Those who work in whatever way for the reconciliation of nations and social justice are thinking and acting in tune with history. For six hundred millions of years, the universe has tended, in an irreversible and immanent movement, toward greater awareness and freedom. In our mind, there is no doubt that the highest form of this awareness and freedom is to be found in cosmic and human unity. Those who work for peace are most efficacious when they work for this unity.

Christians ought to be in the avant garde of those who struggle for the peace of the world. Nothing is more shocking than the chauvinistic and bellicose patriotism of Christians, or to hear priests and even bishops extol the so-called "military virtues" from the pulpit. "Be one as I and the Father are one," Christ said to His apostles. We rightly see in the commandment of the New Alliance the basis of ecclesial unity and the condemnation of all that is divisive among Christians. But we should also remember that the Christian religion is based primarily on the mystery of the Incarnation. Consequently, the commandment of unity applies not only to the spiritual community of the Church, but also to all societies and institutions engaged in promoting the temporal good. "The earth will cease to turn," wrote Teilhard, "before humanity as a whole will cease to organize and unify itself. For if this movement stopped, the universe itself would fail to achieve its plenum."

For my part, I have no trouble admitting that this thought formulates a veritable natural law, a law that accords perfectly with the commandment of the new Alliance just alluded to. But such a law does not operate independently of human collaboration. Man, we repeat with Bergson, is God's co-creator. The law of the universe's general evolution does not favor passivity; rather it determines the direction of our efforts and at the same time assures us that our efforts are not in vain. Teilhard is right when he says that mankind obeys a natural law in aspiring to peace, but he prudently adds that this process of evolution also implies the total engagement of our freedom. Faith in peace must never be separated from faith in man.

If what we have said above is true, then all Christians should have the greatest sympathy for pacifist movements. At least ideally, these movements are in conformity with what we have recognized as God's explicit will as well as with the laws of the spirit's evolution. It is embarrassing to hear officials of the Church speak disparagingly of pacifism. If it were a mere dream then the Gospel would be, too. If pacifists are to be criticized, it is in terms of the means they choose and not the ideal of peace that they pursue heroically.

13

On Christian Resignation

In *The Divine Milieu* we read: "Christian resignation is sincerely considered, and blamed, by many honest people as one of the most dangerously soporofic elements of the religious opium." This is hardly an exaggeration. The majority of both believers and unbelievers understand resignation to be a passive attitude in the face of evil, whether injustice or physical or moral suffering.

In the time of our grandfathers, the greatest obstacle to the evangelization of the world was thought to be religious dogmas. The man of the nineteenth century believed fanatically and naïvely in reason. He was proud to consider himself a "rational animal" and respected only what was rationally grounded. The many scientific discoveries of the age strengthened his hope that human reason would one day resolve all problems and bring peace and happiness to men. Social psychology can readily understand how the conditions of the time led to the view that reason was the only criterion of truth. Now the Christian dogmas, particularly as they have been presented since the Council of Trent, contain much that escapes reason and seems even to flagrantly contradict it. Most of the dogmas were rejected because they could not be explained by biological or physiological laws, laws that were held to be the definitive expression of all truth. At the same time, historical criticism questioned the existence of Christ. Today, it is difficult to understand the confusion that befell the Christians of that era who were strongly attached to their faith. Vehement arguments between my Christian grandmother and my rationalist grandfather remain one of the most vivid memories of my childhood. Each new scientific discovery seemed to further confuse the Christians and furnish the rationalists with new arguments. In the name of this kind of rationality, an Ernest Renan, for example, prophesied around 1880 that in fifty years Christianity would be definitely dead and merely of historical interest.

This confidence in reason seems strange to the educated man today. Not much of this old-fashioned rational optimism is left. Rationalism, not Christianity, is dead fifty years after Renan made his prediction. Of course, classical Christian apologetics had little to do with its demise. The cause must be sought rather in the internal contradictions and the practical failure of the social order based exclusively on reason. This shook the faith of the rationalist. Rationalist pride gave way to skepticism, even despair, because the vaunted light of reason proved incapable of preserving mankind from war or establishing a perfect reign of justice, and because the discovery of atomic energy endangers man's very future. But in our opinion, the pessimism of today is just as naïve as the optimism of yesterday. Reason is as active as ever; but it is more aware of its limitations. Unlike the rationalists of the nineteenth century, scientists today readily admit the tentative nature of much of their work. They even admit that some areas of reality may never be accessible to scientific exploration. Too, we are aware that scientific progress does not automatically increase the happiness of man.

Because of this reversal in the mentality of modern man, there are now few educated men who oppose Christianity for rational reasons. Likewise there are not many who convert to Christianity because they are convinced that Christian dogma does not contradict their rational certitudes. I ofen have occasion to chat with young unbelievers about religion in general and Christianity in particular. They rarely object that the Christian dogmas are absurd, that they are a stumbling block to reason. Most are willing to concede that belief in something rationally undemonstrable is not *a priori* shocking. Most of our contemporaries are little interested in whether there are two or three persons in God, whether the Real Presence must be understood physically or symbolically or whether the proofs for the historical Christ are contestable or not. Even papal infallibility, so recently such a bone of contention, occasions little discussion.

I understand this mentality only too well. It was substantially my own. An old but highly educated priest was surprised to read in one

of my books that I never had any trouble believing in the dogmas of
the Church. But that is a fact. Ever since I became a Christian I
have believed in all the Church's dogmas, even the most recent. The
reason is, I think, that I belong to a different generation. The
modernist crisis did not touch me. Consequently, my psyche is
differently structured, and for that reason my problems are to be
found at another level.

Teilhard de Chardin is undoubtedly right when he says that an
important part of contemporary humanity has the impression that
the Christian religion no longer corresponds to the ideal of life
shared by educated men. As long as they remain so convinced no
argument will convert them to Christianity. Either they will remain
outspoken critics of Christianity, or they will be indifferent to it.
Christians who believe that their religion has an essential message
for humanity do not have the right to hide behind their certitudes
and accuse others of bad faith or partisan blindness. They must ask
themselves in all sincerity if their way of life and methods of presenting the message of Christ are really in accord with the spirit of the
Gospel.

When I first became a Catholic, I often heard this remark in
respect to the evil in the world: "We must resign ourselves!" I
remember a sermon I heard shortly after my conversion. The pastor
was fulminating against a strike that had just been called in a local
factory. He said that Christian workers who took part in it lacked
faith in God by taking this means of getting better working hours
and salaries. They should know, the good pastor went on, that the
Church has always taught resignation before the inevitable evils
and injustices of the world. They are a result of original sin, and
perfect justice will be found only in heaven. This sermon disturbed
me very much. I wondered what such a religion could give me.

Happily, few Christians would adopt such an attitude toward
social injustices today. Nonetheless, many Christians fail to understand that obedience to God's will calls for active collaboration
rather than resignation.

The Christian never has the right to retreat before the assaults of
evil—whether war, poverty, sickness, ignorance, or injustice. He is by
vocation the ally of all who think that man has the duty to become
part of the process of evolutionary creation and to struggle to overcome evil. Of course, the Christian knows that final victory over

evil will not take place in time. Did not Christ say that the poor (the sick, the weak, the victims of injustice) will always be with us? We have, for example, nearly conquered tuberculosis, but cancer and nervous disorders are on the increase. Yet this is no argument for resignation. The men who found the cure for tuberculosis made an incontestable contribution to mankind. Their efforts would have been legitimate even had they failed.

The same is true of the fight against social injustices. Those who are inclined to idealize the past sometimes say that the serfs and slaves of yesteryear were happier than the free workers of today. This could be partially true. Certain African nations have more troubles today than they did under colonialism. But I don't think this is grounds for arguing that they should have resigned themselves to foreign domination and not undertaken the struggle for independence. If we admit that slavery and colonial domination are evils from the point of view of human dignity, passive resignation to such evils would be a betrayal of the creative élan that tends ineluctably towards higher forms of personalization and freedom.

Nor should we resign ourselves to the new forms of evil that have replaced the old, such as cancer, neurosis, the condition of the proletariat, and the disorder that exists in many recently liberated countries. We must always fight against evil. This does not strike me as a pessimistic stance. I find it rather exciting, for there is no danger that life will become boring or monotonous. Imagine for a moment that the communist utopia became a reality. Humanity would live in so perfect a society that there would be nothing to change or improve. This I think would be an unhappy state of affairs, for it would be the static perfection of a society of termites and not the perfection of a human and always perfectible society. I know many young people who were born to wealth and are afflicted with serious mental illnesses precisely because they feel no purpose in their lives, that there is nothing to conquer or create, that all their desires and aspirations were satisfied even before they were aware of what they were. Paradise is a beautiful concept, but not for us wayfarers on earth. When Christ said the poor will always be with us, I think He meant that there would always be evils to fight against.

The evangelical counsel to become perfect as the heavenly Father is perfect is synonymous with the obligation to fight against evil.

Although we shall never attain such perfection, we are not for that reason permitted to resign ourselves to our imperfections. The perfection of God represents a beckoning ideal and will forever condemn him who says: Now I have arrived; it is finished. We see this illustrated very well in the lives of the saints. The world admires them for their perfection, but they never considered themselves perfect. They were only too aware of their imperfections, because they were more aware than other men of God's perfection; consequently, they never rested on their laurels.

Still, the word "resignation" has deep meaning for us. There is such a thing as Christian resignation. Supposing we have done everything possible to make a creative contribution in the circumstances of our lives; yet our efforts have fallen far short of our ideals. Our weakness may well tempt us to despair. There may be a strong temptation to give it all up. Given the fact that we are human, this is a terrible temptation. I might have thought I was a genius or a hero, but experience proves that I am neither. It would, therefore, be altogether natural to consider myself a nothing, to abandon all efforts and resign myself to the daily grind under the guise of "Christian resignation."

Fortunately, true Christian resignation has nothing in common with such a defeatist attitude. The former consists in the humble and courageous recognition of the truth. Granted, I may be neither a genius nor a hero; it does not follow that I am a mere nothing. I am a man, more or less gifted, more or less strong. Realism demands that I forsake unrealizable goals. Life is not a dream. This kind of realistic resignation implies that I should put whatever talents I have in the service of attainable goals. True Christian resignation urges me to adopt a radically active attitude toward life. This is the condition of efficacy; for action is efficacious only if we renounce impossible dreams and undertake goals that are within the realm of possibility.

I recall a discussion with a group of Protestant and Catholic theologians. I was trying to make my conception of Christian resignation clear to them. A young priest, whom I knew to be of strong character as well as very apostolic, cried out in indignation: "I see you profess an activist religion." Most of the others present shared this indignation. In vain did I try to answer their objections. I believe that all religion, especially the Christian religion, should be activist, if that word is to be understood in the sense of "action." The glorification of action is of the very essence of Christianity. Goethe's Faust is quite right to translate the first sentence of St. John's Gospel, In the beginning was the Word, as "in the beginning was action." St. James makes the same point in his epistle: "Put the Word into practice." Moreover, the first chapter of Genesis reveals a creative, not a static God. God commanded things to be, and they were. Nor does the example of Christ mean anything else. His words and His action were inseparable. Indeed, He offered His actions as the proof of His teaching. The contemplation of Christian mystics must not be interpreted as a renunciation of the active life. As a matter of fact, for the greatest of the mystics, contemplation was not passive, but a very active participation in the creative activity of God and the redemptive activity of Christ. Instinctively, Christians have always shunned any form of quietism, however great may have been the temptation to repose in the sweetness of divine love. By their works shall the disciples of Christ be recognized.

14

Detachment Through Transcendence

"To create and organize material energy, whether in the realm of truth or beauty," wrote Teilhard de Chardin in *The Divine Milieu*, "is an interior torment which lifts him who attempts it to the level of a peaceful and fulfilled life where the vice of egoism lurks. To perform creditably in this world we must continually seek better ways of doing things, whether in industry, art or the intellectual life." However partisan we may be to a religion of action, we are quite aware that the life of man is more than action. At the center of our faith is the paschal mystery. But we do not forget that Good Friday played a decisive role in salvation history; consequently, any authentically Christian life must honor the paschal mystery. We love the world and play as active a role as possible in creatively developing it. But the more intense and efficacious our activity is, the more we become aware of the inadequacies of life in this world and all temporal activity. We learn from Genesis that God, on the evening of each day of creation, regarded His work with satisfaction, and after all was completed He rested. This touching narrative tells us nothing about God, for as we said earlier, God creates continually. But it reveals something profound about the human psyche.

As soon as man creates or acquires something, he wants to possess the fruits of his labor. But the Christian who freely accepts the grandiose mission of being God's co-creator, knows that he will never be able to enjoy the fruits of his labor. He must always strive further and higher, which means that he must never be content with any given level of achievement. He must be detached from all worldly goods. Passionate attachment to the world and detachment from the world are, in our opinion, two moments of the same existential dialectic.

Christ said to his disciples: "You are in but not of the world." Over the centuries, this counsel of detachment has been variously interpreted. The early Christian communities, which expected the imminent return of the Lord, saw in it an invitation to renounce all activity and passively await the coming of Christ. But these communities, which we often take to be the perfect model of Christian social life, had a very brief existence. Not that they were wrong; they merely had a truncated view of history. They pooled their goods, produced nothing, and logically enough, one day had nothing.

The Christians of the Middle Ages adopted a very different attitude. At that time, the Church, more for historical than religious reasons, was engaged in building a *Christian world*. Emperors and kings held their authority and dignity from the pope, the Vicar of Christ. Bishops and abbots exercised temporal power. Monks were in charge of education and very often of economic activities. The guilds were at once professional unions and religious fraternities. In a word, medieval society was quite worldly, although theological distinctions made it possible for them not to love the world.

Eventually, medieval civilization fell apart under the weight of its own internal contradictions. We are not concerned here with the following epoch of the Renaissance. Intellectual and spiritual confusion was then so great that even the best of Christians did not know what attitude they should adopt toward the world. Exteriorly, the medieval theocracy seemed to survive; but it was so secularized, even at the Holy See, that there was nothing specifically Christian in it.

In a somewhat simplistic manner, we might consider the present attitude of Christians toward the world and history the result of the Reformation, the Counter Reformation, Jansenism, and Pietism. The world of the Renaissance was so removed from the spirit of the Gospel that such pious men as Luther, Calvin, Ignatius, and Pascal were practically constrained to view the world and Christianity as enemies. Because of this, they were inclined to preach the duty of detachment from the world and the things of this world. They granted that the Christian had a role to play in this world; but he should not take it very seriously. All terrestrial activities had as their end to promote the kingdom of God. Thus, the medieval confusion between the temporal and the religious was replaced by a radical separation of the two orders.

The result of this state of affairs was lamentable. Christianity was not present at the birth of modern science. Far from supporting progress, the Church saw in it a serious danger to the faith. Descartes, Galileo, Copernicus, and so many other masters of the modern world were condemned by the Church. Nor was Christianity present at the birth of capitalism; consequently, it could not protect the poor and weak against its abuses. This eventually led to the separation of the working class from the Church, which Pius XI was to lament so bitterly.

In our opinion, detachment from the world, as it has been understood for the past three or four centuries, flagrantly contradicts the Gospel. Was it not written that Christ so loved the world as to sacrifice His own life for it? The detachment to which all Christians are obliged concerns only our egocentric behavior toward the world. We must never consider any achievement definitive or as properly belonging to us. We must always be ready to detach ourselves from what has been achieved in order to create and discover something new.

I am not thinking primarily of material goods. Detachment from these is generally easy enough for men who have reached any degree of existential authenticity. But it is difficult to detach ourselves from the goods of the spirit. Let us take the example of a scientist who has, after long years and arduous effort, elaborated a system that in all ways seems superior to previous systems. He naturally will be inclined to assume proprietor's rights over his creation. Yet the true scientist must be the servant rather than the proprietor of truth and conduct himself accordingly. He must remain open to other approaches to the truth, even though this means that his own system will be subject to criticism and transformation; indeed he may have to renounce it altogether. However great our successes and conquests appear to us, we must never forget that there is always the possibility and the duty to push forward, to seek yet further.

The Christian must not be detached from work, research, and creativity, but from passivity, laziness, and complacency. And anyone who has ever tried it knows that this is just as difficult as any other form of detachment.

15

Only He Who Has Can Give

"Nemo dat quod not habet," we read in *The Divine Milieu.* "There is no odoriferous smoke without incense, no sacrifice without a victim. How could man give himself to God if he did not exist? What could be gained by detachment if he has empty hands?"

The Christian is often put in the position of having to choose between activity and passivity, between life and death, between growth or nongrowth, between possession or renunciation. From an existential point of view, these are false choices. Life does not confront us with such contrary choices; rather it develops according to the rules of a concrete dialectic comprising successive moments.

I have no doubt that the Christian must strive to be successful in life, even in the temporal domain. Otherwise, the world and time would lose their concrete meaning for him and the pessimistic existentialism of Jean Paul Sartre, which holds life to be absurd, would carry the day. The Christian not only has the right but the duty to develop and enrich himself humanly. I have always found it surprising that the parable of the talents is not exploited more in sermons. On the other hand, the parables of the lilies of the field and the rich young man, always interpreted to mean that the good Christian should abandon all worldy preoccupations, are referred to frequently.

This perversion of Christ's teaching about worldly activity and values began many centuries ago. The *Fioretti* of St. Francis, for example, recounts the story of brother Leo who one day asked the learned St. Bonaventure: "Is it possible for a poor washer-woman to have a higher place in heaven than you, Brother Bonaventure?" The latter answered that that might very well be the case. However, in reality things are not as simple as Brother Leo might have imagined. If he thought that one becomes more pleasing to God by renouncing one's talents to carry out more modest tasks, then he made a very serious mistake. It is a mistake that has been frequently made in the history of Christianity.

God was under no obligation to make us his co-creators. He could have bestowed an ultimate perfection on the world the day He created it. Or He could intervene in a new creation each moment. But the Christian God is a historical God. We know that He in fact acted differently than He could have metaphysically. Instead of giving nature a final perfection he endowed it with immanent laws that guide the evolution and many revolutions of the universe. Moreover, he gave man the capacity to grow in such a manner that he can take an active and conscious part in evolutionary creation. It follows that each time man conducts himself passively, he is unfaithful to his vocation as co-creator.

This should be obvious to anyone who has meditated upon the parable of the talents. In the past, and to some extent today, this parable was understood in a purely "spiritual" sense. The talents were said to signify the grace of God that would be increased through good works interpreted exclusively as prayer, penance, and the like. We do not deny the validity of such works. But temporal works are equally valid. There are some Christians who think, strangely enough, that social progress will diminish their possibility of caring for the sick and poor and thus of collecting merits in God's eyes. I think that the hostility of some Christians toward social progress is motivated by this kind of fear. I know of one pious organization that explicitly urges its members to care for the needy not out of any compassion for their plight, but solely to accumulate merit in God's eyes! Small wonder such a religion holds so little appeal for contemporary man. Such egoism is a sign of infantilism.

We grant that supernatural grace is very important. But it is far from being the only talent God gives us. The light of reason, the strength of liberty, and the body are also gifts. They too come from God and must be multiplied. One wonders, given the doctrine of the Incarnation, whether the distinction between the natural and the supernatural can be anything more than a notional distinction. Since all has been sanctified, it makes no sense to talk of the merely profane.

From a rigorously objective point of view, who is the greater benefactor of mankind: He who gives the beggar a little money and bread, or the man who consecrates his life to the discovery of new techniques and methods by which the lives of many might be qualitatively improved? The two are not mutually exclusive. But we must make it clear that the professional is in a position to exercise as much charity as the good sister who looks after the sick. Since the Second World War, we have become more conscious of the disparity in wealth between the West and the underdeveloped nations. Shouldn't the Christian peoples of the West be scandalized that two-thirds of the world goes hungry? This state of affairs is far more dangerous for the peace of the world and the future of Christianity than, say, communist propaganda. In fact, such propaganda is effective precisely because Christians have failed to carry out the evangelical counsel of loving their neighbor. Individual contributions will not solve this problem; periodic collections are mere stop gaps. Only the talents of statesmen, economists, businessmen, technicians, and scientists can meet the gigantic needs of mankind today. Their talents must be enlisted in truly constructive programs for the future.

One can still admire the example of St. Francis who renounced his paternal fortune and became a poor monk. In fact, similar gestures would not be without value today. But we must not forget that times have changed. An industrialist, for example, would not be following God's will if he sold his business, distributed his profits to the poor, and entered a monastery. To be an authentic co-creator with God at this stage of history would require that the industrialist remain in his factory, even expand it. Conversion should change in the first instance not our activity, but the direction of our activity. Nor would a morning offering be of much use in this context. Too often such good intentions conceal much hypocrisy, whether conscious or unconscious. The spiritual justification of the industrialist's business would be satisfying the needs of mankind by his profits. The same is true of any profession. Neither the thinker nor the researcher, the artist nor the writer is obliged to renounce his profession to become pleasing to God.

No Christian has the right to flee temporal commitment. He can find joy and fulfillment in temporal activity. This should be obvious, yet large numbers are not convinced of it. They feel secretly guilty if they experience any natural satisfaction. It isn't often today that a young wife, say, would confess sexual pleasure as a sin. But the depth psychologist knows that many unconscious auto-punishments are occasioned by such pleasure. How often, too, do we hear people refuse to take credit for something because they enjoy it?

I am convinced that this reluctance to accept life's pleasures is unnatural and abnormal. We read in *Genesis* that God rejoiced after each day's creation because He found His work "good." Must we not imitate the divine model in this as in all other things. There is no Biblical justification for sourpusses. Some years ago young factory workers in a Paris suburb conducted an interesting experiment. Having become interested in the Christian religion by contact with the priest-workers, they adopted the habit of going into churches to see if faith in eternal life could be discerned on the faces of the worshipers. They were sadly deceived, for in almost all cases they found churchgoers a glum lot. "Why do Christians always seem to be in mourning?" they asked. "Don't they believe in Christ's resurrection?"

Perhaps other ages may have had more justification for a pessimistic attitude. But that is not the case today. Most men think that the world is a good place and that man has a worthwhile mission to accomplish in it. True, many are anguished by the general insecurity of our times. But all, even the most outspoken atheists, think that the Christian, if he really believes in the promises of his religion, should be above such doubts and anxiety. We must recognize that unbelievers expect this of us. All things contribute to the fulfillment of the universe—*etiam peccata,* even sin as St. Augustine said; the Christian has less right than anyone to find life sad. Unbelievers often think that Christians attach more importance to Good Friday than to Easter. It was because Teilhard de Chardin stressed the paschal theme that his writings found such response.

However, the Christian optimist, like any other mature man, must be always ready to sacrifice his enjoyment of life, indeed life itself if necessary, for a higher end. Only the man who accepts values for which he is ready to die can truly enjoy life. We always admire examples of supreme generosity. In this way, we learn something about Christian detachment that is perfectly reconcilable with the most passionate attachment. At all times, it is a question not only of living, but of living more intensely.

Thus, in the Christian life there is no conflict between love and life and detachment or renunciation. I am thinking at the moment of all the renunciations that sickness, old age, and finally death impose upon us. André Malraux has written that man is the only animal who knows he is mortal, and it is for this reason that life is so despairing. The Christian, on the other hand, knows that death itself can be very meaningful, and for this reason life is neither despairing nor absurd for him.

16

The Cross of Christ

"Too often," Teilhard de Chardin wrote in *The Divine Milieu,* "the Cross is presented for our adoration less as a sublime end which we can attain only by transcending ourselves than as a symbol of sorrow, restriction and repression." There seems to be an apparently insurmountable misunderstanding between a religion centered on the crucified Son of God and a world primarily concerned with success and efficacy. This misunderstanding antedates the "modern world." The conflict seems to be as old as Christianity itself. The "world" as such would appear to be in formal conflict with the religion of the Cross. The Gospel recounts the scandal and deception many experienced when Christ did not accept the ironic challenge to come down from the Cross and thus prove that He was truly the Son of the Most High. The pagans of the Greco-Roman world were often willing to listen to the Apostles so long as they spoke of Christ's miracles; but as soon as the Crucifixion was mentioned, they turned their backs in derision. The world, whether Jewish or Greek, ancient or modern, cannot think of God except as triumphant. When ancient mythologies spoke of the death of a god, they presented it as something wondrous. There was never an instance of the shameful kind of death Christ underwent.

Only the pious Middle Ages accepted Christ's death on the Cross as almost "normal." The mentality of that age was inclined to think that without such a death there would be something essential lacking in Christianity. Historically, Christ's death has played an effective role in Christianity; any Christian is perfectly free to make it the central point of his religious meditations. Unfortunately, the later

Middle Ages, the Age of the Counter Reform, and Jansenism stressed the mystery of the Cross so exclusively that men lost sight of the fact that it was after all only one of the means of eternal salvation; Christ could just as well have saved humanity in some other way. There is every reason to see in the Crucifixion a marvelous proof of God's love for His creatures, [but what was a free Divine choice should not be invested with some kind of philosophical necessity.]

The most active and probably the sanest part of humanity today has a very high estimation of temporal life; indeed, they may often overestimate the value, joys, and pleasures of this life. Many Christians fall into this category, and it seems likely that their number will increase as they become more conscious of their vocation as co-creators with God. But their religious training has warned them against the dangers of life in the world; Sunday sermons urge them to take up the Cross of Christ and follow Him in renouncing this world. The dramatic character of many such sermons may temporarily touch their hearts; but most Christians soon come to the uncomfortable conclusion that religion and life are radically heterogenous and irreconcilable. Consequently, many of them ignore the mystery of the Cross altogether since it seems to play no positive role in their lives.

As for unbelievers, how can they be expected to make sense out of a mystery that even Christians have difficulty understanding? They can only see in it the sign and the symbol of Christianity's radical hostility toward the world and the condemnation of all human efforts. Modern existentialist philosophy, which professes that life is absurd, seems to them very similar to the religion of the Cross. They do not understand why we should mortify the flesh and the spirit and consider all ascesis not only meaningless, but harmful to happiness and health. Many of our contemporaries agree with Nietzsche's vehement attacks on the religion of the Cross, although most men today would not formulate their arguments so bitterly.

There can be no question of eliminating the mystery of the Cross from the Christian economy merely because it represents a stumbling block to modern man. Revelation cannot be accommodated to men's sense of what is acceptable or not. Quite the contrary; it is our firm conviction that Christianity must always be presented in its entirety, for only as such can it become the soul of the contemporary and future world. Now the mystery of the Cross is incontestably an integral part of total Revelation. Those who contemplate the crucified Christ are not unfaithful to Revelation. The object of their contemplation is in accord with a sorrowful reality. I would only remind them, in case they have forgotten, that the realism of the Cross does not exhaust the whole mystery of the Crucifixion. I am of the opinion that Oriental art has captured the total meaning of this event much better than the art of the West. In Byzantine art, the crucified Christ appears more majestic and divine, less humiliated and defeated. The Eastern artist seems more aware that the Crucified had already conquered evil and death. His arms are extended to embrace all of creation and offer it redeemed to His Father. Western art, with its emphasis on the brutal physical details of the Crucifixion, may be more in keeping with the letter of history; nonetheless, I think the Orientals have grasped the deep meaning of the mystery of Redemption much better than have our Lenten preachers, with their touching and pious images that they so misuse.

It goes without saying that the Christian cannot be insensitive to the sufferings of Christ on the Cross. We know for a fact that His suffering was motivated by love for us, and we are, therefore, perfectly justified in seeing some proportion between the intensity of his suffering and the immensity of his love. But we also know that Christ's sufferings terminated as soon as He died. It is not, therefore, strictly accurate to speak of His sufferings as though they were still going on. What continues, what is eternal, is the effect of these sufferings—which is to say, the Redemption. Thus, the Christian has no reason to be sad even on Good Friday. Although that day calls for special meditation on Christ's physical suffering, we should never forget that He has resurrected and sits in glory at His Father's right hand. Furthermore, by His suffering, He prepared a place for us with Him by the Father's side.

I am inclined to stress the triumph and glory of the Crucifixion. The Cross is not a shameful symbol; it is the sign of redemptive love. Henceforth, everything stands in a new relationship to God. And I do not think I am wrong in believing that many of our contemporaries, if they were to accept the above interpretation, could see an affirmation of life in the mystery of the Cross.

The mystery of the Cross is one with the mystery of Redemption.

Both are one with the mystery of the Incarnation. We become sons of God, and all of creation is transposed to the supernatural order as a result of the Incarnation. In company with many theologians and mystics, I do not see original sin as the cause of the Incarnation. It is quite possible that the Son of God would have become incarnate had there been no original calamity. It seems, indeed, that something important would be lacking to creative love without this "hominization" of God. Because of the *de facto* state of sin, the Redemption was necessary to complete the Incarnation and to effect the supernaturalization of a disordered world.

These observations do not totally clarify the mystery of the Cross. Our human conceptions of justice and equity cannot comprehend the disparity between man's sin and the price the Son of God paid for our Redemption. It is scarcely conceivable that He did so to stir our imaginations, to make us see more clearly the gravity of sin and the immensity of divine love. If this were the case, we would be more inclined to speak of God's ineffable severity than of His infinite love.

I find the explanation that Adam's sin must be evaluated not in terms of him who committed it but in terms of the dignity of the one offended very unsatisfactory. To admit that man's sin could really hurt God would be to form a very low estimate of Divine sovereignty. Such a perspective seems too grossly anthropomorphic. However immanent God is in His creation, His transcendence is nonetheless absolute. We can only speak of God's joys and sufferings allegorically. Moreover, since Christ was God, the least of His actions necessarily had infinite value. Any one of them would have been sufficient to compensate for all the sins of man.

It is possible that the Word of God, in becoming man, wanted to experience the whole negative dimension of human existence. From this point of view, we need not attribute the fact that Christ chose Judas Iscariot as a disciple to some divine decree. The circumstances surrounding the Crucifixion—Pilate's cowardice, the blindness of the religious leaders, etc.—were no more *willed* by God than the suffering of each one of us. Judas could have resisted the temptation to betray Christ. Pilate could have resisted the cries of the populace. The worth of the Redemption would have been in no way compromised, even if Christ had terminated His life in happy old age. God's positive will was that the Word repair the disorder caused by men's sin and reconcile fallen humanity with its Creator, thus making it possible for us to attain the supernatural order for which the immensity of divine love has destined us. The various modalities of Christ's life, including the Crucifixion, can be considered accidental.

17

Wonders and Miracles

"The Christian miracle," writes Teilhard de Chardin in his *Introduction to the Christian Life*," is now understood by us less as "prodigies of detail" than as vital signs of our faith in Christ." Nothing, it would seem, better reveals the changes that have taken place in the human psyche than the difference between men's attitude toward miracles before the advent of the scientific era and the attitude presently dominant. Formerly, miracles could be neither too numerous nor too dramatic. Those related in the Gospels were considered insufficient. Pious authors compensated for this shortcoming by imaginatively recasting the life of Christ. They attributed miracles to Christ that compared favorably with the legends and mythologies of other religions. After all, Christ could not appear inferior to the gods of Homer! The authors of these stories probably intended nothing more than edification; but in the minds of their readers, it became increasingly difficult to distinguish the apocryphal from the authentic.

Too, the official biographies of the saints were too uninspiring for people who were strangers to such stimulating media as movies, radio, and television. A few years ago, I made a study of books written on the lives of Saints Dominic and Francis between the thirteenth and seventeenth centuries. I was surprised, and somewhat moved, to discover that miracles, prophecies, and other prodigies of the two saints multiplied with each new generation. It was as though the hagiographers had entered a veritable competition. The accumulation of relics is motivated by the same psychological needs. Early Christians had an insatiable appetite for the dramatic.

It is thus not surprising that the theology and apologetics of the Middle Ages made miracles and prophecy the two essential proofs of the true religion. Christ is God, they argued, because He worked miracles in support of His teaching and all of His prophecies were realized. The Catholic Church is the true Church of God because miracles are constantly being worked by her saints. They for the most part ignored the fact that other religions made similar claims.

The psychology of modern man is very different. Miracles, far from constituting a proof of religion, form one of the chief obstacles to it. This is at least true for educated men; the masses in many countries seem almost medieval in their thirst for the miraculous. In any event, miracles are stressed much less today both in theology and in preaching.

It is not our intention to cast doubt on the miracles that have been authenticated by the Church, especially those recounted in the Gospel. Since I believe in God I have no difficulty admitting that His creative activity is not necessarily subjugated to the laws of nature. As Teilhard de Chardin once said: "Christianity would no longer be Christianity if we did not think, however confusedly, that under God's influence cosmic determinism and chance are finalized and animated by our union with God and our prayer." It is, of course, true that many miracles in the Gospel must be understood symbolically since they are more didactic parables than facts.

Neither I nor many other educated believers today believe in Christ because of His miracles. It is rather because we believe in Christ that we admit at least the possibility of His miracles. Without our faith in Christ it would be easy to explain the prodigies recounted by the evangelists in purely natural terms and thus satisfy our rational curiosity. Moreover, my faith would be in no way affected had the Gospel made no mention of miracles. It would if anything be stronger since certain embarrassing questions would no longer disturb me.

The only miracle that is truly an integral part of the Christian faith and that all Christians must accept is the Resurrection of Christ. If we read the *Acts of the Apostles,* it becomes clear that this was the only miracle that served as a major argument in apostolic preaching. By the miracle of the Resurrection, Christ conquered death and evil and effectively *proved* His divinity. But I do not find it necessary for my faith to believe that He resurrected physically.

I have visited many of the celebrated shrines of Europe. Whether the Virgin appeared physically to, say, Bernardette is of no great importance. What matters is that devotion to Christ's mother be encouraged. This fact alone is sufficient to justify the existence of the great shrines; they are in some sense saints. I remember Father Lagrange, the celebrated exegete and historian, once saying that as a historian he could scarcely give credence to the legend that Mary Magdalen once lived in the grotto of Sainte Baume. But, he added, "whether she lived there or not is unimportant. In a real sense she lives there now because she is venerated and her friendship for Christ honored." Modern man can understand shrines and pilgrimages in this spiritual sense; he has no desire or need to justify them historically or scientifically.

In this sense, too, I have great respect for the best known shrine of our day, Lourdes. But I think I can say without disrespect to the Virgin or the faithful who believe in the miracles that are said to be worked there, that they hold no interest for me whatsoever. All the better if people recover their health there; I would be very happy if that happened to me. But when I visit Lourdes, I am neither surprised nor disappointed if I witness no miracles. I pray as well as I can without them. Even if the apparitions to Bernadette were more psychic than physical, this shrine has been hallowed by the faith of millions of Christians who have prayed there. Had I witnessed a genuine miracle, it would probably have neither strengthened nor weakened my faith. I am, like many others, disturbed by the commercial exploitation that goes on at Lourdes. But that is a very different problem.

I enjoy reading the many legendary accounts in the lives of the saints. Their historical truth does not interest me. As a psychologist, I know that legend can be as "true" as history. Poetry is a literary form that is as legitimate and at least as true as statistics.

18

Eternal Life

"In itself," wrote Teilhard de Chardin in *How I Believe,* "the problem of personal immortality concerns me little. I shall be content if the best part of me becomes forever part of something more beautiful and greater than me." These lines played an important role in the progressive and not always easy development of my Christian faith. When I asked the Catholic Church for baptism at the age of twenty-seven, I was not seeking the salvation of my soul. I was not even sure I had a soul; and in any case, the matter was of no interest to me. I had broken with the Communist Party a year before, and my life had lost all sense of purpose and direction. I no longer understood anything about the world and could justify neither my own life nor that of others. In the Christian faith I regained a sense of purpose. I naturally accepted Christian revelation as a whole and categorically refused to pick and choose among its dogmas and customs. For that reason I believed that I was endowed with a spiritual soul and that it was destined for eternal happiness. On the *existential* level, this belief had no influence on my life or behavior. How I acted had nothing to do with the salvation of my soul.

Frequently my co-religionists reproached me for not saying more in my books and conferences about salvation, thus giving the impression that I was interested only in the temporal aspects of Christianity. I once said in a talk that the individual salvation of my soul didn't interest me. In the following days, I received several letters from pantheists who saw in me a kindred spirit. But, as I have already pointed out, I am not a pantheist. I am quite convinced that eternal life represents a highly personal reality. But I am not satisfied with the way in which this doctrine is usually expounded. Eternal life is explained in too individualistic a perspective, as though the sole purpose of man on this earth was to merit *his* eternal salvation. In my early days in the Church, I was often given the impression, a very embarrassing one for me, that the good Christian was only concerned with this. The spiritual life was a matter of avoiding the temptations of life in the world.

No mature person today would accept that conception of eternal life. We are too conscious of the thousand bonds that join us with other men and with the whole universe. Because of this, it is absolutely impossible to imagine ourselves separated from this communitarian network, even in heaven. I would find it easier to believe in the dissolution of individual consciousness in a collective cosmic consciousness than in a rigorously individualistic salvation. At any rate, neither I nor many other men today would be shocked if Christianity professed such a dissolution of the individual in the cosmic. On the contrary, if this were the case many of our difficulties would be solved.

In reality, Christian revelation offers a much better solution than cosmic dissolution. It effectively and synthetically reconciles universalism and personalism. All the relevant evangelical parables represent eternal life in the form of community life: weddings, feasts, etc. Yet those invited to these celebrations retain their identity. In St. Paul's words, they have put on the "new man," but they remain nonetheless the same persons we knew on this earth.

Thanks to Teilhard de Chardin I understand that there is no conflict between my faith in a personal immortality on the one hand, and on the other, my strong faith in the human and cosmic community. I will always remain convinced that the essential thing is not the salvation of my soul, but the fulfillment of creation. I conceive of eschatology as a cosmic event and quite secondarily as an individual event. But, again following Teilhard, there can be no doubt that the process of cosmic maturation is accompanied by increasing personal consciousness. If eternity necessitated the dissolution of personality, it would not be the fulfillment of evolutionary creation. The development of personality and the development of the cosmos go hand in hand. The destruction of one would imply the destruction of the other. But God does not destroy His creation.

The promises of Christian revelation justify our hope in eternal life. But here again a static ideology has appreciably distorted the truth. If we ask Christians: "How do you conceive of eternal life?" they will most generally answer: "As eternal rest." If we understand the term "rest" as the absence of all anguish and suffering, it would be accurate but quite incomplete; it would say more what eternal life is not than what it is. In practice we think of rest as the absence of activity, somewhat comparable to retirement. The only occupation of the elect, so it is said, would be to sing pious hymns.

It is not difficult to understand that this conception of the kingdom of heaven is not very exciting for modern man. The state of retirement can hardly be considered an existential ideal. Men cannot be expected to adopt a monastic pattern of life. Professionally, I have observed how paralyzing retirement can be for men who enjoyed their work. As long as they were active they felt useful and happy. After a few months of retirement, they generally become oppressed; many literally begin a slow death. Early retirement is creating a serious sociological and psychological problem today. In my opinion, it can be resolved only if retirement is seen as a new and more interesting form of life, rather than the end of everything that makes life worthwhlie.

We have said repeatedly that life is essentially activity, that man realizes his vocation principally through action. In this he finds his highest joy. Eternity is not the destruction of the temporal, but its fulfillment. Either eternal life consists in the most sublime form of activity, or we must admit that there is no personal salvation, that the end of life in this world implies the dissolution of individuals in an impersonal whole. But, as we have often noted, evolution tends toward increasing personalization, and according to Christian revelation, immortality must be interpreted as personal. It follows that personal salvation cannot be a passive state of rest.

As a person matures, the activity of the spirit plays a greater role in his life. For this reason, we may suppose that the activity of eternal life will be highly spiritual. The two most important spiritual activities are love and knowledge. They also afford us our most intense happiness. The man who spends his life avoiding temptation and lets his faculties of love and knowledge atrophy is preparing himself for eternal life very poorly. On the other hand, he who during his life on earth passionately seeks the truth and develops his capacity for love to the maximum already anticipates the joys of heaven.

Thus the Christian sees death as the passage to a higher form of life. The essence of terrestrial life, which is to say primarily action and progress, will also be the essence of eternal life. There is no danger of boredom! The first object of our love and knowledge is in fact God Himself. Since He is infinite Truth and Love, there will always be a place for greater progress and deeper intensity in our efforts to know and love Him better. The many mansions in the Heavenly Kingdom is a way of saying that there are many degrees in our love and knowledge of God.

19

The Holy Church

Teilhard de Chardin's lifelong difficulties with the Church are well known. Instead of being hailed as a creative pioneer in bridging the gap between Christianity and the modern world, he was accused of destroying the "deposit of faith" and treated accordingly. Even his superiors gave him little support. In the last years of his life, when the whole scientific world honored him as one of its most eminent representatives, his ecclesiastical superiors still thought it advisable to "exile" him from France and forbade him from participating in scientific congresses and research. It is hardly surprising that such measures caused much bitterness, although much more for his friends and disciples than for Teilhard himself. On several occasions, rumors circulated that the Jesuit scholar was about to break with his Order and even the Church itself. In 1929, when these rumors were most ripe, Teilhard wrote categorically: "I would betray the 'world' if I attempted to evade the place assigned to me. Rest assured then that the idea of leaving the Order has never crossed my mind. The Company is *my* point of insertion and action in the universe." He remained faithful to the end.

In the early centuries of the Church, pagans were rarely converted because they were doctrinally convinced; rather, they were attracted in almost every case by the Christian way of life. At the time of my own conversion, I knew very little about Christian dogmas. I was converted as a result of my reading and personal contacts with a number of outstanding Christians. I later learned about the Church's dogmas, and I never had any difficulty accepting them. Yet it was not long before I experienced the difficulties involved in remaining faithful to a Church that I truly believe, despite everything, to be the Church of Christ.

For me and many other educated men, the Church today is the greatest obstacle to faith. I know many deeply spiritual men and women who have read and meditated upon Teilhard's writings and other avant-garde Catholic authors. They feel in perfect accord with these writers and would admit, furthermore, that only the Christian faith can give their lives the meaning and depth they crave. They are even disposed to accept the Church's dogmas and discipline if they were explained to them in an intelligent manner. But, alas, the Church so often gives the impression that she is not interested in understanding the modern world and its spiritual needs.

In traditionally Catholic circles, many outstanding men, spiritually mature and thirsting for religious truth, are put off by the Church's doctrinal and disciplinary measures. We have only to recall, by way of example, the encyclical *Humani Generis,* the condemnation of the priest-workers, and the rebukes administered to Teilhard de Chardin and other eminent Christian thinkers. How anachronistic seem so many of the pastoral letters and allocutions we have read in recent years! If a Cardinal Saliège or a Pope John received such sympathetic response, it was more by reason of their *style* of writing, speaking, and acting than any novelty of doctrine. But the fact that a pope who wanted to remain a "humble country pastor" failed to rid the Vatican of its outdated machinery and had to be carried to the inaugural session of Vatican II on the famous *sedia* is proof that the administrative body of the Church has not understood that we have entered a new phase of universal history and that the Church must strive to become the soul of the new world in the making. Thus, it is quite normal that the Church take a position on the great problems of our age, but in doing so she should take into account the psychological and sociological conditions of the modern world. This was unhappily not the case in a recent statement on birth control by the French episcopacy, rightly considered one of the more progressive. They spoke as if nothing had changed in the world since Biblical times. On the other hand, John XXIII's last two encyclicals—*Mater et Magistra* and *Pacem in Terris*—indicated what the role of the Church in our society could be.

Many scholars were surprised that Teilhard de Chardin remained faithful to his order and the Church. During the controversy over *Humani Generis*, I and my progressive Catholic friends were often asked: "Why do you stay in the Church? You would be much more effective if you could act with more freedom."

A "perfect" Church is, of course, an old temptation. A succession of Montanists, Fraticelli, Cartharists, Jansenists, and many other sects claimed to be among the "pure." But if the Church of God were comprised only of saints a terrible problem would arise. What would authorize us to count ourselves among the members of such a Church? We would be overwhelmed by the enormous distance between us and perfection. An objective analysis of the "perfectionist complex" reveals that the true source of the temptation to erect a "perfect" Church is to be found in a natural tendency toward the ready-made and static. We are not yet convinced that the perfection of all created beings in space and in history is never given, but is always in a state of perpetual becoming. The origin of the Church is certainly divine; but she is subject to the general law of evolution. And as we have frequently pointed out, spiritual evolution is not realized mechanically, but calls for our active collaboration. The perfection of the Church is not to be found in the past, but in the future. However great our admiration for primitive Christianity, there can be no question of a return to the past. Our efforts must be centered on the Christianity of the future, on the era of man come of age.

I do not criticize the Church for her inevitable imperfections, but because, at least at the administrative level, she acts with such contempt and hostility toward the evolution of the world and the maturation of mankind. But this does not strike me as a serious reason for breaking with the Church. Our painful awareness of the distance separating the Church and the modern world urges us to do what we can to make it possible for the Church to accomplish her mission in the history of the universe better. Two thousand years of history has proved that Church "reform" has a much better chance for success if it is undertaken from within. Those Christians who have left the Church in the hope of living their faith better and making greater contributions to the renaissance of Christianity have in almost all cases been condemned to total inefficacy. Some abandoned the faith altogether; others returned to the fold. We can, therefore, only make ours the words of

Teilhard: by not accepting the place God has assigned us in the building up of His Church, we would betray the universe.

I am not of course arguing that there is no sanctity or genuine love of God outside of Catholicism. There are many excellent Christians in other Churches. Furthermore, I consider Mahatma Gandhi one of the greatest saints of our time, and I know many fervent servants of God among the Hindus, Moslems, and other non-Christian religions. I can affirm this with perfect orthodoxy since it has always been recognized that the visible Church is but a part of the whole Church. But since God has willed me to discover the visible Church and join it, my place is there.

Sometime back an eminent German Catholic visited me. Partly as a result of reading my books, he had become keenly aware of the Church's deficiencies in the modern world. He wrote a book proposing some very intelligent reforms. To assure its success, he sent copies to the Pope, the Papal Nuncio, his bishop, Chancellor Adenauer, the Minister of Defense Strauss, and other important Catholic figures. None of them acknowledged receiving the volume; in all likelihood, none of them read it. The author committed a serious error that goes against all the laws of cosmic evolution. If we are convinced that we have a mission to accomplish in the world or in the Church, we can expect little help from popes, bishops, or so-called Christian heads of state. The great in the Church are too convinced that they have no need of our light, that they know best what is to be done—and of course they are frequently right. We should begin at the bottom; the masses should be the object of our concern. Only much later, perhaps centuries later, will the great recognize the fruits of our labor. Theoretically, a reform could be decreed from on high. But in this case it would very likely fail to grasp the heart of man.